1959 U.S.

YEARBOOK

ISBN: 9781790533237

This book gives a fascinating and informative insight into life in the United States in 1959. It includes everything from the most popular music of the year to the cost of a buying a new house. Additionally there are chapters covering people in high office, the best-selling films of the year and all the main news and events. Want to know who won the World Series or which U.S. personalities were born in 1959? All this and much more awaits you within.

INDEX

FIRST EDITION

1959

January
S	M	T	W	T	F	S
				1	2	3
4	5	6	7	8	9	10
11	12	13	14	15	16	17
18	19	20	21	22	23	24
25	26	27	28	29	30	31

◑:2 ●:9 ◐:16 ○:24 ◑:31

February
S	M	T	W	T	F	S
1	2	3	4	5	6	7
8	9	10	11	12	13	14
15	16	17	18	19	20	21
22	23	24	25	26	27	28

●:7 ◐:15 ○:23

March
S	M	T	W	T	F	S
1	2	3	4	5	6	7
8	9	10	11	12	13	14
15	16	17	18	19	20	21
22	23	24	25	26	27	28
29	30	31				

◑:1 ●:9 ◐:17 ○:24 ◑:31

April
S	M	T	W	T	F	S
			1	2	3	4
5	6	7	8	9	10	11
12	13	14	15	16	17	18
19	20	21	22	23	24	25
26	27	28	29	30		

●:7 ◐:16 ○:23 ◑:29

May
S	M	T	W	T	F	S
					1	2
3	4	5	6	7	8	9
10	11	12	13	14	15	16
17	18	19	20	21	22	23
24	25	26	27	28	29	30
31						

●:7 ◐:15 ○:22 ◑:29

June
S	M	T	W	T	F	S
	1	2	3	4	5	6
7	8	9	10	11	12	13
14	15	16	17	18	19	20
21	22	23	24	25	26	27
28	29	30				

●:6 ◐:14 ○:20 ◑:27

July
S	M	T	W	T	F	S
			1	2	3	4
5	6	7	8	9	10	11
12	13	14	15	16	17	18
19	20	21	22	23	24	25
26	27	28	29	30	31	

●:5 ◐:13 ○:19 ◑:27

August
S	M	T	W	T	F	S
						1
2	3	4	5	6	7	8
9	10	11	12	13	14	15
16	17	18	19	20	21	22
23	24	25	26	27	28	29
30	31					

●:4 ◐:11 ○:18 ◑:26

September
S	M	T	W	T	F	S
		1	2	3	4	5
6	7	8	9	10	11	12
13	14	15	16	17	18	19
20	21	22	23	24	25	26
27	28	29	30			

●:2 ◐:9 ○:16 ◑:24

October
S	M	T	W	T	F	S
				1	2	3
4	5	6	7	8	9	10
11	12	13	14	15	16	17
18	19	20	21	22	23	24
25	26	27	28	29	30	31

●:2 ◐:9 ○:16 ◑:24 ●:31

November
S	M	T	W	T	F	S
1	2	3	4	5	6	7
8	9	10	11	12	13	14
15	16	17	18	19	20	21
22	23	24	25	26	27	28
29	30					

◐:7 ○:15 ◑:23 ●:30

December
S	M	T	W	T	F	S
		1	2	3	4	5
6	7	8	9	10	11	12
13	14	15	16	17	18	19
20	21	22	23	24	25	26
27	28	29	30	31		

◐:6 ○:14 ◑:22 ●:29

PEOPLE IN HIGH OFFICE

President Dwight D. Eisenhower
January 20, 1953 - January 20, 1961 / Republican Party

Born October 14, 1890, Eisenhower was a former 5 star general in the U.S. Army during WWII and the first Supreme Commander of NATO. He served as the 34th President of the United States and died January 22, 1973.

85th & 86th United States Congress

Vice President	Richard Nixon
Chief Justice	Earl Warren
Speaker of the House	Sam Rayburn
Senate Majority Leader	Lyndon B. Johnson

U.S. Flag - 48 stars (1912-1959)

United Kingdom

Monarch
Queen Elizabeth II
February 6, 1952 - Present

Prime Minister
Harold Macmillan
January 10, 1957 - October 19, 1963

Australia

Canada

Ireland

Prime Minister
Sir Robert Menzies
December 19, 1949 -
January 26, 1966

Prime Minister
John Diefenbaker
June 21, 1957 -
April 22, 1963

Taoiseach of Ireland
Éamon de Valera
March 20, 1957 -
June 23, 1959

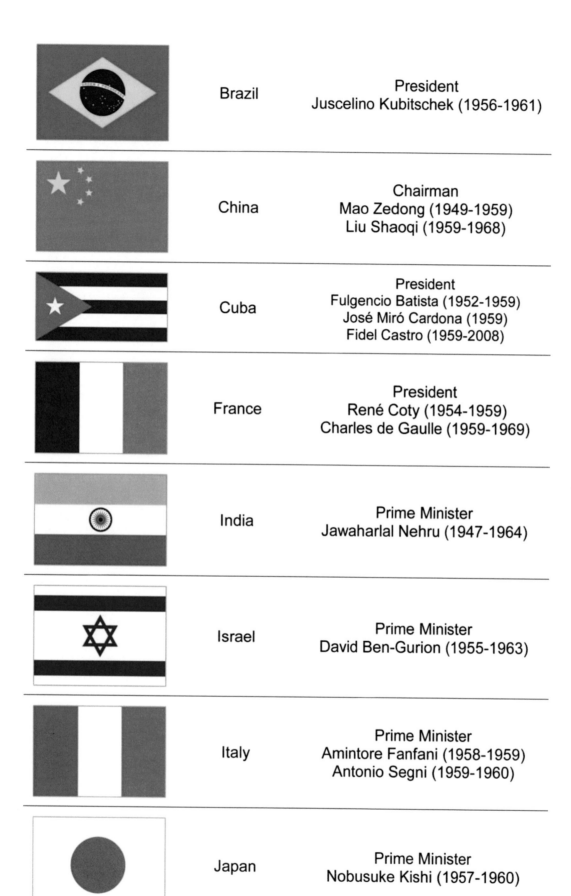

	Brazil	President Juscelino Kubitschek (1956-1961)
	China	Chairman Mao Zedong (1949-1959) Liu Shaoqi (1959-1968)
	Cuba	President Fulgencio Batista (1952-1959) José Miró Cardona (1959) Fidel Castro (1959-2008)
	France	President René Coty (1954-1959) Charles de Gaulle (1959-1969)
	India	Prime Minister Jawaharlal Nehru (1947-1964)
	Israel	Prime Minister David Ben-Gurion (1955-1963)
	Italy	Prime Minister Amintore Fanfani (1958-1959) Antonio Segni (1959-1960)
	Japan	Prime Minister Nobusuke Kishi (1957-1960)

 Mexico

President
Adolfo López Mateos (1958-1964)

 New Zealand

Prime Minister
Walter Nash (1957-1960)

 Pakistan

President
Ayub Khan (1958-1969)

 South Africa

Prime Minister
Hendrik Verwoerd (1958-1966)

 Soviet Union

Communist Party Leader
Nikita Khrushchev (1953-1964)

 Spain

President
Francisco Franco (1938-1973)

 Turkey

Prime Minister
Adnan Menderes (1950-1960)

 West Germany

Chancellor
Konrad Adenauer (1949-1963)

U.S. NEWS & EVENTS

JAN

2   CBS Radio cuts four soap operas: Backstage Wife, Our Gal Sunday, The Road Of Life, and This Is Nora Drake.

3   Alaska is admitted as the 49th U.S. state.

7   The United States recognizes the new Cuban government of Fidel Castro just six days after the fall of Fulgencio Batista's dictatorship in Cuba. Despite fears that Castro, whose rebel army helped to overthrow Batista, might have communist leanings, the U.S. government believed that it could work with the new regime and protect American interests in Cuba.

January 9 - Rawhide, a Western TV series starring Eric Fleming and Clint Eastwood, premieres on CBS. The show spanned 7½ years, 8 seasons and 217 black-and-white episodes. It was the sixth-longest-running American television Western, exceeded only by 8 years of Wagon Train, 9 years of The Virginian, 14 years of Bonanza, 18 years of Death Valley Days, and 20 years of Gunsmoke.

12   The record company Motown is founded by Berry Gordy Jr. as Tamla Records; it was incorporated as Motown Record Corporation a year later on the April 14, 1960.

22   Knox Mine Disaster: Water breaches the River Slope Mine in Greater Pittston's Port Griffith, Pennsylvania; 12 miners are killed. The disaster is widely credited with single-handedly killing the mining industry in the Northern Anthracite Region of Pennsylvania.

25   The first American transcontinental commercial jet flight is made by an American Airlines Boeing 707, from Los Angeles to New York.

29   Walt Disney Animation Studios release the film Sleeping Beauty Los Angeles, California. It is the first animated film to be photographed using the Super Technirama 70 widescreen process, as well as the second full-length animated feature film to be filmed in anamorphic widescreen, following Disney's own Lady and the Tramp four years earlier.

FEB

2   Vince Lombardi signs a contract to coach Green Bay Packers. Whilst there he would lead the team to five NFL Championships in seven years, including the first two Super Bowls at the conclusion of the 1966 and 1967 NFL seasons; following his sudden death from cancer in 1970 the Super Bowl trophy was named in his honor. Lombardi is considered by many to be the greatest coach in football history and was enshrined in the Pro Football Hall of Fame in 1971, the year after his death.

3   American Airlines Flight 320, en route from Chicago Midway International Airport to New York City's LaGuardia Airport, crashes into the East River with the loss of 65 lives.

Portraits, left to right; Buddy Holly, The Big Bopper and Ritchie Valens.

February 3 - A chartered plane transporting musicians Buddy Holly, Ritchie Valens and The Big Bopper crashes in foggy conditions near Clear Lake, Iowa, killing all 4 occupants on board including pilot Roger Peterson. The tragedy is later termed 'The Day The Music Died', and was popularised in Don McLean's 1972 song American Pie.

6	At Cape Canaveral, Florida, the first successful test firing of the U.S. Titan intercontinental ballistic missile (ICBM) is accomplished.
10	A F4 tornado crosses through parts of the St. Louis Metropolitan Area causing the deaths of 21 people and injuring 345.
17	The United States Navy launch Vanguard 2 to measure cloud cover and to provide information on the density of the atmosphere. As the world's first weather satellite it is an important part of the space race between the U.S. and the Soviet Union.
20	Rock and roll guitarist Jimi Hendrix, aged 16, plays his first gig in the Temple De Hirsch synagogue basement, Seattle. He is fired from the band between sets due to his wild playing.
27	During a basketball game between Boston Celtics and Minneapolis Lakers, Boston Celtic Bob Cousy sets NBA record with 28 assists; the game finished 173-139 to the Celtics. This record has since been beaten twice, firstly in February 1978 by Kevin Porter of the New Jersey Nets with 29 assists, and then by Scott Skiles of Orlando Magic in December 1990 with 30 assists.
29	Lee Petty wins the inaugural Daytona 500 in front of 41,921 spectators. Petty completed the 200-lap race with an average speed of 135.521-mph.

1	The USS Tuscaloosa, USS New Orleans, USS Tennessee and USS West Virginia are all struck from the Naval Vessel Register.
3	Pioneer 4, the first U.S. probe to escape from Earth's gravity on a lunar flyby trajectory and enter a solar orbit, is launched from Cape Canaveral. The pressure to succeed with this lunar mission had been enormous after the Soviet Luna 1 probe had conducted the first successful flyby of the Moon on January 3.
5	The 16th Golden Globes are held honoring the best in film for 1958; The Defiant Ones, David Niven and Susan Hayward are amongst the winners.
6	The 11th Emmy Awards, to honor the best in television of the year, are held at the Moulin Rouge Nightclub in Hollywood, California. Playhouse 90, The Jack Benny Show, Perry Como and Raymond Burr are amongst the winners.

8	Groucho, Chico and Harpo Marx make their final TV appearance together in The Incredible Jewel Robbery. It was an instalment of CBS General Electric Theater anthology series, which ran from 1953 to 1962, and was hosted by Ronald Reagan.
11	A Raisin in the Sun by Lorraine Hansberry opens on Broadway in New York City. The story tells of a black family's experiences in the Washington Park Subdivision of Chicago's Woodlawn neighborhood as they attempt to "better" themselves with an insurance payout following the death of the father. The New York Drama Critics' Circle named it the best play of 1959.
18	President Eisenhower signs in to law the Admission Act dissolving the Territory of Hawaii and establishing the State of Hawaii as the 50th state to be admitted into the Union. Hawaii's statehood became effective on August 21, 1959.
18	Boston Celtic's Bill Sharman begins a record of 56 straight free-throws during the NBA Playoffs.
24	At the Institute of Radio Engineers' annual trade show at the New York Coliseum in New York City, Texas Instruments, one of the U.S.'s leading electronics firms, introduces the solid integrated circuit (aka the microchip).
31	Busch Gardens, a 335-acre animal theme park in Tampa, Florida, is dedicated and opens its gates.

APR

6	The 31st Academy Awards ceremony is held at Pantages Theatre, Hollywood, California, to honor the best films of 1958. The Oscar winners included David Niven, Susan Hayward and the film Gigi.

April 9 - NASA announces its selection of the 'Mercury Seven', seven military pilots who were to take part in the United States' first human space flight program, Project Mercury. These first U.S. astronauts were Alan Shepard, John Glenn, Walter Schirra, Donald Slayton, Virgil 'Gus' Grissom, L. Gordon Cooper, and M. Scott Carpenter. Many of the men would also later go on to take part in future NASA projects such as the Gemini program and the Apollo program. Some notable achievements by the Mercury Seven included Alan Shepard becoming the first American in space and John Glenn becoming the first American to orbit the Earth.

Photos; 1. NASA group portrait of the 'Original Seven' astronauts from the Mercury program as they pose in front of an Air Force jet in Florida (1963); from left, Scott Carpenter, Gordon Cooper, John Glenn, Gus Grissom, Wally Schirra, Alan Shepherd, and Deke Slayton - 2. The Mercury Seven astronauts in 1960.

APR

9	The 1959 NBA World Championship Series sees the Boston Celtics sweep the Minneapolis Lakers in 4 games.
15	The Secretary of State John Foster Dulles resigns due to failing health. Dulles dies on May 24, 1959 at the age of 71; he was posthumously awarded the Medal of Freedom and the Sylvanus Thayer Award.
25	The St. Lawrence Seaway linking the North American Great Lakes and the Atlantic Ocean opens to shipping.

MAY

1	Floyd Patterson knocks out Englishman Brian London in 11 rounds during his 4th World Heavyweight Boxing title defence at the Fairgrounds Coliseum in Indianapolis, Indiana.
4	The first Annual Grammy Awards are held to recognise musical accomplishments of performers for the year 1958. Two separate ceremonies were held simultaneously in Beverly Hills and New York City, with Count Basie, Domenico Modugno, Henry Mancini, Ella Fitzgerald and Perry Como amongst the winners.
7	93,103 people crowded in to the LA Coliseum for 'Roy Campanella Night' setting an attendance record for a game between major-league teams. The game was arranged to lessen the costs involved in Campanella's medical care after a car accident on January 28, 1958. The exhibition game raised approximately $60,000 for him and saw the Dodgers beat the Yankees 6-2.
12	Yankee catcher Yogi Berra's errorless streak of 148 games comes to an end when he commits an error on his 34th birthday.
25	The Supreme Court, in a suit filed by African-American prize-fighter Joseph Dorsey Jr., rules that Louisiana prohibiting black-white boxing is unconstitutional.

JUN

5	Bob Dylan (born Robert Allen Zimmerman) graduates from Hibbing High School in Minnesota.

June 8 - The USS Barbero assists the United States Postal Service with its first and only delivery of 'Missile Mail' off the northern Florida coast. The mail, consisting entirely of commemorative postal covers, arrived at the Naval Auxiliary Air Station, Mayport, Florida after 22 minutes aboard a Regulus cruise missile.

9	The United States submarine USS George Washington (SSBN-598) is launched at Groton, Connecticut, and is the first submarine to carry ballistic missiles (16 Polaris A-1 missiles). The submarine was commissioned on December 30, 1959.

JUN

23	Convicted Manhattan Project spy Klaus Fuchs is released from a British prison after only 9 years and 4 months of a 14 year sentence. He promptly emigrates to Dresden, East Germany where he resumes a scientific career.
26	Queen Elizabeth II and President Dwight D. Eisenhower formally open the St. Lawrence Seaway with a short cruise aboard the Royal Yacht Britannia, after addressing crowds in Saint-Lambert, Quebec.
26	Sweden's Ingemar Johansson defeats Floyd Patterson, after flooring him seven times in the third round, to take The Ring and World Heavyweight boxing titles at Yankee Stadium in New York City.
30	Benjamin O. Davis Jr. becomes the first black Major General in US Air Force.

JUL

8	Major Dale R. Buis and Master Sergeant Chester M. Ovnand become the first Americans killed in action in Vietnam. Both were advisors supporting the South Vietnamese in their fight against the North.
15	500,000 members of the labor union United Steel Workers of America (USWA) go on strike. Lasting for 116 days the strike leads to significant importation of foreign steel for the first time in U.S. history.
24	With the admission of Alaska as the 49th U.S. state earlier in the year, the 49-star flag of the United States debuts in Philadelphia, Pennsylvania.

July 24 - At the opening of the American National Exhibition in Moscow, U.S. Vice President Richard Nixon and USSR Premier Nikita Khrushchev have what becomes known as the 'kitchen debate'. In the kitchen of a model home built in the exhibition, Nixon and Khrushchev went at each other with voices rising and fingers pointing as they jousted over which system was superior, communism or capitalism.

AUG

7	A fire at the Gerretsen Building Supply Company in Roseburg, Oregon ignites a truck carrying a 2 ton load of dynamite and 4½ tons of ammonium nitrate. The subsequent blast kills 14, levels 8 city blocks, creates a crater 52 feet in diameter and 12 feet deep, and causes $12 million worth of damage.
17	An earthquake measuring 7.2 on the Moment Magnitude Scale strikes Madison Canyon, an area to the west of Yellowstone National Park. Labeled the Hebgen Lake earthquake it caused a huge landslide which blocked the flow of the Madison River and created Quake Lake. The quake, the strongest and deadliest earthquake to ever hit Montana, resulted in over 28 fatalities and damage estimated at $11 million.

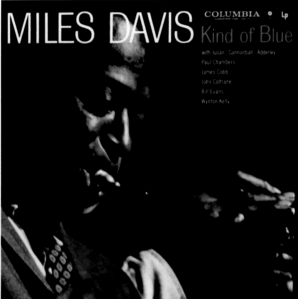

August 17 - Trumpeter Miles Davis' influential jazz album Kind of Blue is released. It is regarded by many critics as jazz's greatest record and its influence on music, including jazz, rock, and classical genres, has led writers to also deem it one of the most influential albums ever recorded. The album was one of fifty recordings chosen in 2002 by the Library of Congress to be added to the National Recording Registry, and in 2003 it was ranked number 12 on Rolling Stone magazine's list of the 500 greatest albums of all time. It is not only Davis's best-selling album but also the best-selling jazz record of all time with sales in excess of four million copies.

SEP

11	Edward Kennedy 'Duke' Ellington wins the Springarn Medal, awarded annually by the National Association for the Advancement of Colored People (NAACP), for his "outstanding and unique musical achievements".
12	The television western series Bonanza premieres on NBC and becomes one of the first weekly television series to be broadcast completely in color. Set in the 1860s it centers on the wealthy Cartwright family who live in the area of Virginia City, Nevada. Bonanza is NBC's longest-running western (1959-1973), lasting 14 seasons and 431 episodes.

OCT

2	Rod Serling's classic anthology series The Twilight Zone premieres on CBS. The series, shot entirely in black and white, ran on CBS for five seasons from 1959 to 1964.
5	The IBM 1401, considered to be the Model T Ford of the computer industry because it was mass-produced and because of its sales volume, is announced by IBM. Some 12,000 units would be manufactured with many later leased or resold after they were replaced with newer technology. The 1401 was eventually withdrawn on the February 8, 1971.
6	The half hour crime series 'Philip Marlowe' debuts on ABC-TV. Starring Philip Carey as Marlowe, the show lasts just 1 season and features 26 episodes.
21	In New York City the Solomon R. Guggenheim Museum (designed by Frank Lloyd Wright) opens to the public. It is the permanent home of a continuously expanding collection of Impressionist, Post-Impressionist, early Modern and contemporary art, and attracts over 1 million visitors per year.

NOV

1	In a game between the Montreal Canadiens and New York Rangers of the National Hockey League (NHL), Canadiens goaltender Jacques Plante, after being struck in the face by a shot from Andy Bathgate, becomes the first goaltender to use a mask.
15	Four members of the Clutter family of Holcomb, Kansas are brutally murdered by Richard 'Dick' Hickock and Perry Smith. The crime was later to be made famous by Truman Capote in his 1966 non-fiction novel 'In Cold Blood'.
18	MGM's widescreen, multimillion-dollar, Technicolor version of Ben-Hur, starring Charlton Heston, premieres in New York City. It is critically acclaimed and eventually wins 11 Academy Awards; a record which has only ever been equalled by Titanic (1997) and The Lord of the Rings: The Return of the King (2003).
29	The second Grammy Awards are held to recognise musical accomplishments of performers for the year 1959. Hosted by Meredith Willson, this marked the first televised Grammy Award ceremony and saw Duke Ellington, Bobby Darin, Ella Fitzgerald and Frank Sinatra amongst the winners.

DEC

| 4 | Little Joe 2, a mission to test the Mercury space capsule, carries Sam the monkey into space. The flight was launched from Wallops Island, Virginia, U.S. and flew to an altitude of 55 miles. After 11 minutes and 6 seconds it returned to Earth before being recovered in the Atlantic Ocean by USS Borie. |
| 13 | Three years after it's first telecast, MGM's The Wizard of Oz is shown on television for the second time. It gains an even larger viewing audience than its first outing and persuades CBS to make it an annual tradition. |

1959 EXTRA

THE NEW *ELECTRIC* POWERED AUTOMOBILE

The National Union Electric Company introduces the $3600, 36-volt Henney Kilowatt.

The Henney Kilowatt was an electric car introduced in the United States in 1959. The car used some body parts from the Renault Dauphine and had a top speed of 40-mph, with a range of 40 miles on a full charge; an improved 72-volt model was introduced in 1960 with a top speed of 60 miles an hour and a range of 60 miles. Only 47 cars were sold over the two model years, 32 to electrical utility companies and 15 to the general public. The Kilowatt has been called the world's first mass production electric car and today it is estimated that there are only between four and eight still in existence.

1959 NOTABLE U.S. DEATHS

Jan 21	Carl Dean Switzer (b. August 7, 1927) - Singer, guide, breeder of hunting dogs and child actor. He is best remembered for appearing as Alfalfa in the Our Gang comedy short films series (aka The Little Rascals) during the 1930s.
Jan 21	Cecil Blount DeMille (b. August 12, 1881) - Filmmaker who between 1914 and 1958 made a total of 70 features. He is acknowledged as a founding father of cinema in the U.S. and is one of the most commercially successful producer-directors in film history. His films were distinguished by their epic scale and by his cinematic showmanship.
Feb 3	Jiles Perry 'J. P.' Richardson Jr. (b. October 24, 1930) - Musician, songwriter and disc jockey better known as The Big Bopper. His rockabilly look, style, voice and exuberant personality made him an early rock and roll star. He is best known for his 1958 recording of Chantilly Lace.
Feb 3	Charles Hardin Holley (b. September 7, 1936) - Musician, singer-songwriter and record producer otherwise known as Buddy Holly. He was spotted by Nashville scout Eddie Crandall (who helped him get a contract with Decca Records) after opening for Bill Haley and His Comets in October 1955. Holly would then go on to become a central and pioneering figure of mid-1950s rock and roll.
Feb 3	Richard Steven Valenzuela (b. May 13, 1941) - Singer, songwriter and guitarist known professionally as Ritchie Valens. A rock and roll pioneer and a forefather of the Chicano rock movement. Valens' recording career lasted just eight months before his death, aged just 17, in the plane crash that also killed Buddy Holly and The Big Bopper.
Feb 22	Helen Parrish (b. March 12, 1924) - Film actress who first started in movies at the age of 2 and has a star on the Motion Pictures section of the Hollywood Walk of Fame.

Lou Costello (right) with Bud Abbott - one of most popular comedy duos of the 20th century.

March 3, 1959 - Louis Francis Cristillo (b. March 6, 1906) - Actor of radio, stage, television and film, known professionally as Lou Costello. He is best remembered for his comedy double act of 'Abbott and Costello' with Bud Abbott. They started in burlesque before showcasing their routines on radio, Broadway, and in 36 Hollywood films between 1940 and 1956. Costello would always play a bumbling character opposite Abbott's straight man, and was known for his catchphrases 'Heeeeyyy, Abbott!' and 'I'm a baaaaad boy!'

CONTINUED

Mar 4	Maxwell Warburn Long (b. October 16, 1878) - Athlete and winner of 400 meter dash at the 1900 Summer Olympics in Paris.
Apr 9	Frank Lloyd Wright (b. June 8, 1867) - Architect, interior designer, writer and educator whose creative period spanned more than 70 years. Wright believed in designing structures that were in harmony with humanity and its environment, a philosophy he called organic architecture. This philosophy was best exemplified by Fallingwater (1935) which the American Institute of Architects named as the 'best all-time work of American architecture'.
Jun 2	Orelia Key Bell (b. April 8, 1864) - Poet whose notable works include Millennium Hymn (1893) and Poems (1895).
Jun 16	George Reeves (b. January 5, 1914) - Actor best known for his role as Clark Kent / Superman in the 1950s television program 'Adventures of Superman'.
Jun 18	Ethel Barrymore (b. Ethel Mae Blythe; August 15, 1879) - Preeminent stage actress whose career spanned six decades and who is often regarded as 'The First Lady of the American Theatre'.
Jun 25	Charles Raymond 'Charlie' Starkweather (b. November 24, 1938) - Teenage spree killer who murdered eleven people in the states of Nebraska and Wyoming. All but one of Starkweather's victims were killed between January 21 and January 29, 1958, the date of his arrest. During the murders committed in 1958 Starkweather was accompanied by his 14-year-old girlfriend Caril Ann Fugate.
Jul 8	Major Dale Richard Buis (b. August 29, 1921) and Master Sergeant Chester Melvin Ovnand (b. September 8, 1914) - The first two Americans killed in Vietnam.
Jul 17	Eleanora Fagan (b. April 7, 1915) - Jazz musician and singer-songwriter who was better known as Billie Holiday. With a career spanning nearly thirty years Holiday had a seminal influence on jazz music and her vocal style pioneered a new way of manipulating phrasing and tempo.
Aug 16	Fleet Admiral William Frederick Halsey Jr., KBE (b. October 30, 1882) - Admiral in the United States Navy during World War II. Known as Bill Halsey or 'Bull' Halsey, he is one of just four individuals to have attained the rank of Fleet Admiral in the U.S. Navy.
Oct 7	Mario Lanza (b. Alfredo Arnold Cocozza; January 31, 1921) - American tenor and actor of Italian ancestry. Lanza was a Hollywood film star during the late 1940s and 1950s and at the time of his death in 1959 was the world's most famous tenor.
Oct 14	Errol Leslie Flynn (b. June 20, 1909) - Australian-born actor who became a U.S. citizen in 1942. Flynn was known for his romantic swashbuckler roles in Hollywood films as well as his frequent on-screen partnerships with Olivia de Havilland.
Oct 16	George Catlett Marshall Jr. (b. December 31, 1880) - Statesman and soldier who rose through the U.S. Army to become Chief of Staff under presidents Franklin D. Roosevelt and Harry S. Truman, and then served as Secretary of State and Secretary of Defense under Truman. Winston Churchill lauded Marshall as the 'organizer of victory' for his leadership of the Allied victory in World War II, although Marshall declined a final field leadership position that went to his protégé, later U.S. President, Dwight D. Eisenhower. After the war, as Secretary of State, Marshall advocated a significant U.S. economic and political commitment to post-war European recovery, including the Marshall Plan that bore his name. In recognition of this work he was awarded the Nobel Peace Prize in 1953.
Nov 21	Maximilian Adelbert 'Max' Baer (b. February 11, 1909) - Boxer of the 1930s and one-time Heavyweight Champion of the World; Baer was also a referee and had an occasional role on film and television. He was the brother of heavyweight boxing contender Buddy Baer and father of actor Max Baer Jr. (best known as Jethro Bodine on The Beverly Hillbillies). Baer is rated No.22 on Ring Magazine's list of 100 greatest punchers of all time.
Dec 19	Walter Washington Green Williams (b. November 14, 1854) - Debunked soldier who had claimed to be the last surviving veteran of the American Civil War.

1. | January 2 - The USSR launches Mechta (Luna 1) which becomes the first craft to leave Earth's gravity on its intended route to impact the Moon. Due to a programming error the duration of the upper stage burn was incorrectly set; Luna 1 missed its target passing within 3,725-miles of the Moon's surface. As a consequence of this it became the first spacecraft to be placed in a heliocentric orbit and today it still remains in orbit around the Sun between Earth and Mars.

2. | January 8 - Charles de Gaulle is inaugurated as president of France's 5th Republic.

3. | February 19 - The London and Zürich Agreements (for the constitution of Cyprus) are drafted and agreed, granting Cyprus independence from Britain. Cyprus was accordingly proclaimed an independent state on the August 16, 1960.

4. | March 31 - The Dalai Lama, fleeing the Chinese suppression of a national uprising in Tibet, crosses the border into India after an epic 15-day journey on foot over the Himalayan mountains. Once in India he is granted political asylum.

5. | April 27 - Mao Zedong resigns as Chairman of the People's Republic of China after the disastrous failure of the Great Leap Forward.

6. June 11 - Christopher Cockerell's invention, the Saunders-Roe SR.N1 hovercraft, is officially launched and makes its maiden flight in front of various assembled members of the press. The demonstration received considerable press coverage, the majority of which being largely positive.

On July 25, 1959, the 50th anniversary of Louis Blériot's cross-channel flight, the SR.N1 crossed the English Channel from Calais to Dover in just over two hours; the crew during this crossing consisted of Captain Peter Lamb (pilot), John Chaplin (navigator) and Cockerell himself.

In December 1959, the Duke of Edinburgh visited Saunders-Roe at East Cowes and persuaded the chief test-pilot, Commander Peter Lamb, to allow him to take over the SR.N1's controls. He flew the SR.N1 so fast that he was asked to slow down a little. On examination of the craft afterwards it was found that she had been dished in the bow due to excessive speed, damage that was never allowed to be repaired and was from then on affectionately referred to as the 'Royal Dent'.

7. July 17 - British paleoanthropologist Mary Leakey discovers the partial skull of a new species of early human ancestor, Zinjanthropus boisei or Zinj (now called Paranthropus boisei), that had lived in Africa some 1.75 million years ago.

8. August 8 - Chinese-American reproductive biologist Min Chueh Chang reports the first mammals (a litter of rabbits) grown from ova having undergone in vitro fertilisation and transferred to a surrogate mother.

9. August 26 - The British Motor Corporation introduce the first Morris Mini-Minor, registration number 621 AOK. Designed by Alec Issigonis (pictured) the Mini was produced from 1959 until October 2000 (although BMW, after acquiring the Rover Group in 1994, have retained the rights to continue to build cars using the Mini name). The Mini is considered an icon of 1960s British popular culture and was voted the second most influential car of the 20th century behind the Model T Ford. In total 5.3 million Minis have been sold making it the most popular British car ever made.

10. September 12 - Luna 2 is launched by the USSR and becomes the first spacecraft to reach the surface of the Moon, and the first man-made object to land on another celestial body.

11. September 20 to 27 - Typhoon Vera strikes Japan killing at least 4,000 people. It is the deadliest typhoon in Japanese history and causes damage equivalent to around $5.04 billion today.

12. September 19 - Giuseppe Cocconi and Philip Morrison establish the scientific rationale for SETI with the publishing of their seminal paper 'Searching for Interstellar Communications'.

13. October 4 - The Russian probe Luna 3 sends back the first images of the far side of the Moon. These historic never-before-seen views of the far side of the Moon caused excitement and interest when they were published around the world. They depicted a mountainous terrain with just two dark low-lying regions, very different from the near side of the Moon.

14. October 22 to 28 - The deadliest Pacific hurricane on record kills 1,800 people in Mexico.

15. November 24 - A 150kg meteorite makes a landfall in Azerbaijan. During its descent it was accompanied by a bright blinding flare which illuminated and area of 1,100 sq mi.

16. December 1 - The Antarctic Treaty is signed in Washington by the twelve countries that had been active in the Antarctic region during the previous year; the United States, United Kingdom, Soviet Union, Norway, Japan, New Zealand, South Africa, Belgium, France, Argentina, Chile, and Australia. The purpose of the treaty was to guarantee peaceful use of the uninhabited continent for scientific purposes and global cooperation. The treaty became effective on June 23, 1961 and has since been expanded to include a total of 53 countries.

17. December 11 - Emilio G. Segrè and Owen Chamberlain publish their discovery of the antiproton for which they are both awarded the 1959 Nobel Prize in Physics.

18. Notable releases / inventions from 1959: Mattel release the Barbie Doll, Wilson Greatbatch invents the internal pacemaker, Joseph-Armand Bombardier patents the Ski-Doo snowmobile (originally christened the Ski-Dog, but renamed because of a typographical error that Bombardier decided not to change), and Eveready engineer Lewis Urry invents the long-lasting alkaline battery.

U.S. PERSONALITIES
BORN IN 1959

Susanna Lee Hoffs
January 17, 1959

Vocalist, guitarist and actress who is best known as a co-founder of The Bangles with Debbi and Vicki Peterson. The Bangles' first recorded release was a self-titled EP in 1982 on the Faulty Products Label. The Bangles released their first full album All Over The Place in 1984 on Columbia Records, but their commercial breakthrough came with the album Different Light in 1986 which produced the hit singles 'Manic Monday', 'If She Knew What She Wants', and 'Walk Like an Egyptian'.

Lawrence Julius Taylor
February 4, 1959

Former American football player nicknamed 'L.T.' who played his entire professional career as a linebacker in the NFL for the New York Giants (1981-1993). Taylor won a record three AP NFL Defensive Player Of The Year awards and was named the league's Most Valuable Player (MVP) for his performance during the 1986 season. He was named First-team All-Pro in each of his first nine seasons and is widely considered as one of the greatest players in the history of American football.

John Patrick McEnroe Jr.
February 16, 1959

Retired tennis player often considered among the greatest in the history of the sport. He was known for his shot-making artistry and volleying skills, as well as his confrontational on-court behavior that frequently landed him in trouble. McEnroe was the winner of seven Grand Slam single titles and contributed to five Davis Cup titles for the U.S. He attained the No.1 ranking in both singles and doubles, finishing his career with 77 singles and 78 doubles titles; this remains the highest men's combined total of the Open Era.

Kyle Merritt MacLachlan
February 22, 1959

Actor best known for his role as Dale Cooper in Twin Peaks (1990-1991; 2017) and its film prequel Twin Peaks: Fire Walk With Me (1992). MacLachlan has had prominent roles in a number of television shows during his career including Sex And The City (2000-2002), Desperate Housewives (2006-2012), How I Met Your Mother (2010-2014), Portlandia (2011-2018) and Agents Of S.H.I.E.L.D. (2014-2015). In 1991 he won a Golden Globe Award for Best Actor in a Television Series Drama for his role in Twin Peaks.

David Hyde Pierce
April 3, 1959

Pierce is known for playing the psychiatrist Dr. Niles Crane on the NBC sitcom Frasier, winning four Primetime Emmy Awards for Outstanding Supporting Actor in a Comedy Series during the show's run (he was nominated for the Outstanding Supporting Actor Emmy for a record eleven consecutive years). Pierce also has appeared on and directed for the stage. In 2007 he won the Tony Award for Best Performance by a Leading Actor in a Musical for his performance in the musical Curtains.

Kenneth Brian Edmonds
April 10, 1959

Singer, songwriter and record producer known professionally as Babyface. He has written and produced over 26 No.1 R&B hits throughout his career and has won 11 Grammy Awards. Babyface has also won a total of 51 BMI Awards including the BMI Pop Songwriter Of The Year trophy seven times and a BMI Icon Award at the 6th annual BMI Urban Awards. In 1999 a 25-mile stretch of Interstate 65 that runs through Indianapolis was renamed Kenneth 'Babyface' Edmonds Highway.

Randy Bruce Traywick
May 4, 1959

Country music and Christian country music singer, songwriter, guitarist, and actor known professionally as Randy Travis. Active since 1978, he has recorded 20 studio albums and charted more than 50 singles on the Billboard Hot Country Songs charts, including 16 that reached the No.1 position. He has sold over 25 million records and has won 6 Grammy Awards, 6 CMA Awards, 9 ACM Awards, 10 AMA Awards and 8 Dove Awards. In 2016 Travis was inducted into the Country Music Hall of Fame.

Ronald Mandel Lott
May 8, 1959

Former American professional football player who was a cornerback, free safety, and strong safety in the NFL for fourteen seasons during the 1980s and 1990s. A first-round pick in the 1981 NFL Draft, he played professionally for the San Francisco 49ers, Los Angeles Raiders, New York Jets, and Kansas City Chiefs. Lott was elected into the Pro Football Hall of Fame in 2000 and is widely considered to be one of the best players in NFL history.

Loretta Elizabeth Lynch
May 21, 1959

American lawyer who served as the 83rd Attorney General of the United States, appointed by President Barack Obama in 2015 to succeed Eric Holder. On April 23, 2015, Lynch was confirmed by the Senate by a 56-43 vote, making her the second woman, and the first African-American woman, to be appointed as Attorney General. She was sworn in on April 27, 2015. Previously she held the position for United States Attorney for the Eastern District of New York under both the Clinton and Obama administrations.

Michael Richard Pence
June 7, 1959

Politician and lawyer serving as the 48th and current Vice President of the United States, in office since January 20, 2017. He was previously the 50th Governor of Indiana from 2013 to 2017 and a member of the United States House of Representatives from 2001 to 2013. Pence is the sixth U.S. Vice President from Indiana following Schuyler Colfax (1869-1873), Thomas A. Hendricks (1885), Charles W. Fairbanks (1905-1909), Thomas R. Marshall (1913-1921) and Dan Quayle (1989-1993).

James Brian Hellwig
June 16, 1959 -
April 8, 2014

Professional wrestler who most famously wrestled under the ring name The Ultimate Warrior for the WWF (now WWE) from 1987 to 1991, and again in 1992 and 1996. While in the WWF, Warrior became a two-time WWF Intercontinental Heavyweight Champion and won the WWF World Heavyweight Championship once when he pinned Hulk Hogan in the main event at WrestleMania VI in Toronto, making him the first wrestler to hold both titles concurrently.

Kevin Scott Nash
July 9, 1959

Actor and semi-retired professional wrestler currently signed to WWE under their Legends program. Nash has wrestled under several ring names but is best known for his work under his real name in WCW and TNA. Nash also found success in WWF when in 1994 he won all three titles comprising the WWF Triple Crown. In total Nash has won an impressive 21 championships, including being a five-time world champion and a 12-time world tag team champion.

Richard Stephen 'Richie' Sambora
July 11, 1959

Rock guitarist, singer, songwriter and producer, best known as the lead guitarist of the rock band Bon Jovi for 30 years. Bon Jovi has released 13 studio albums and sold more than 100 million records worldwide making them one of the best-selling American rock bands of all-time. Sambora has also released three solo albums and has been inducted into the Rock and Roll Hall Of Fame as a member of Bon Jovi, and the Songwriters Hall Of Fame with songwriting partner Jon Bon Jovi.

Susana M. Martinez
July 14, 1959

Politician and attorney who is the 31st Governor of New Mexico and was the chair of the Republican Governors Association. Martinez was elected governor on November 2, 2010 and sworn into office on January 1, 2011. She is the first female governor of New Mexico and the first Hispanic female governor in the United States. In 2010 the State Bar of New Mexico named Martinez 'Prosecutor Of The Year' and in 2013 she was named as one of Time magazine's 100 most influential people in the world.

Kevin Spacey Fowler, KBE
July 26, 1959

Actor, producer and singer who began his career as a stage actor during the 1980s before obtaining supporting roles in film and television. He gained critical acclaim in the early 1990s culminating in winning an Academy Award for Best Supporting Actor in The Usual Suspects (1995) and an Academy Award for Best Actor for American Beauty (1999). In Broadway theatre, Spacey won a Tony Award in 1991 for his role in Lost In Yonkers.

Marcia Gay Harden
August 14, 1959

Actress whose film breakthrough was in Miller's Crossing (1990). In the 2000 film Pollock she won the Academy Award for Best Supporting Actress, and in 2003 earned an Academy Award nomination for her performance in the movie Mystic River. Harden made her Broadway debut in 1993 starring in Angels In America. She returned to Broadway in 2009 as Veronica in God of Carnage; her performance won her the Tony Award for Best Actress in a Play.

Earvin 'Magic' Johnson Jr.
August 14, 1959

Retired professional basketball player who played point guard for the Los Angeles Lakers of the NBA for 13 seasons. He won a championship and an NBA Finals Most Valuable Player Award in his rookie season, and won four more championships with the Lakers during the 1980s. Johnson's career achievements include 3 NBA MVP Awards, 9 NBA Finals appearances, 12 All-Star games, and 10 All-NBA First and Second Team nominations. In 1996 Johnson was honored as one of the 50 Greatest Players in NBA History.

Scott Douglas 'Scooter' Altman
August 15, 1959

U.S. Navy Captain, engineer, test pilot and former NASA astronaut who is a veteran of four Space Shuttle missions. He was selected as an astronaut candidate by NASA in December 1994 and after completing a year's training at the Lyndon B. Johnson Space Center went on to log over 40 days in space aboard the Space Shuttles Columbia and Atlantis. Altman retired from NASA in September 2010 to join ASRC Federal Research and Technology Solutions in Greenbelt, Maryland.

Timothy Raines Sr.
September 16, 1959

Professional baseball coach and former player nicknamed 'Rock'. He played as a left fielder in Major League Baseball for six teams from 1979 to 2002 but was best known for his 13 seasons with the Montreal Expos. He is widely regarded as one of the best leadoff hitters and base runners in baseball history. Raines was the 1986 NL batting champion, a seven-time All-Star and four-time stolen base champion. He was elected to the National Baseball Hall Of Fame on January 18, 2017.

Jay Scott Greenspan
September 23, 1959

Actor, voice actor, comedian, and director better known by his stage name Jason Alexander. Alexander is best known for his role as George Costanza in the television series Seinfeld. Other well-known roles include Phillip Stuckey in the film Pretty Woman (1990) and the title character in the animated series Duckman (1994-1997). Alexander has had an active career on stage, appearing in several Broadway musicals including 'Jerome Robbins' Broadway' in 1989, for which he won the Tony Award as Best Leading Actor in a Musical.

Frederick Steven Couples
October 3, 1959

Professional golfer who has competed on the PGA Tour and the PGA Tour Champions. He is a former World No.1 and has won 64 professional tournaments, most notably the Masters Tournament (1992) and the Players Championship (1984, 1996). Couples garnered the nickname 'Boom Boom' for his long accurate driving ability off the tee during the prime of his career. He was inducted into the National Italian-American Sports Hall of Fame in 2007 and the World Golf Hall of Fame in 2013.

Olive Marie Osmond
October 13, 1959

Singer, actress, doll designer and a member of the show business family the Osmonds. Although she was never part of her family's singing group she gained success as a solo country music artist; her best known song is a cover of the country pop ballad 'Paper Roses'. From 1976 to 1979 she and her brother Donny hosted the television variety show Donny & Marie. During the mid-1990s Osmond had a successful run performing Broadway musicals, selling out many major cities and receiving glowing reviews from the critics.

Alfred Matthew 'Weird Al' Yankovic
October 23, 1959

Singer, songwriter, film and record producer, satirist and author. He is known for his humorous songs that make light of popular culture and often parody specific songs by contemporary musical acts. Since his first-aired comedy song in 1976 he has sold more than 12 million albums, recorded more than 150 parody and original songs, and has performed more than 1,000 live shows - his works have earned him four Grammy Awards. His latest album, Mandatory Fun (2014), became his first No.1 album during its debut week.

Allison Brooks Janney
November 19, 1959

Actress whose breakthrough occurred with her portrayal of White House Press Secretary (and later White House Chief of Staff) C.J. Cregg on the NBC political drama The West Wing (1999-2006), for which she received four Primetime Emmy Awards. In 2017, her performance as LaVona Golden in I, Tonya earned her numerous accolades including the Academy Award, Golden Globe Award, Screen Actors Guild Award, Critics' Choice Movie Award, Independent Spirit Award, and BAFTA Award for Best Supporting Actress.

Florence Delorez Griffith-Joyner
December 21, 1959 -
September 21, 1998

Track and field athlete also known as Flo-Jo. At the 1988 Seoul Olympics she won three gold medals and one silver medal, setting world records in both the 100m and 200m races. These records still stand today endorsing her status as the fastest woman of all time. Shortly after the 1988 games she abruptly retired from athletics but remained a pop culture figure through endorsement deals, acting, and designing. The USA Track & Field National Governing Body inducted her into its Hall of Fame in 1995.

Michael Phillip Anderson
December 25, 1959 -
February 1, 2003

U.S. Air Force officer and NASA astronaut. Anderson and his six fellow crew members were killed in the Space Shuttle Columbia disaster when the craft disintegrated during its re-entry into the Earth's atmosphere after a successful 16-day trip to orbit conducting scientific experiments. He served as the payload commander and lieutenant colonel in charge of the science experiments on the Columbia, NASA's oldest shuttle. Anderson was posthumously awarded the Congressional Space Medal of Honor.

Val Edward Kilmer
December 31, 1959

Actor of stage and screen who became popular in the mid-1980s after a string of appearances in comedy films starting with Top Secret! (1984), then the cult classic Real Genius (1985), as well as the military action film Top Gun (1986), the fantasy film Willow (1988), and Doc Holliday in Tombstone (1993). Some of his other notable film roles include Jim Morrison in The Doors (1991), Bruce Wayne / Batman in Batman Forever (1995), Simon Templar in The Saint (1997) and astronaut Robby Gallagher in Red Planet (2000).

1959 TOP 10 SINGLES

Johnny Horton	No.1	The Battle Of New Orleans
Bobby Darin	No.2	Mack The Knife
Lloyd Price	No.3	Personality
Frankie Avalon	No.4	Venus
Paul Anka	No.5	Lonely Boy
Bobby Darin	No.6	Dream Lover
The Browns	No.7	The Three Bells
The Fleetwoods	No.8	Come Softly To Me
Wilbert Harrison	No.9	Kansas City
The Fleetwoods	No.10	Mr. Blue

Johnny Horton
The Battle Of New Orleans

Label:	Written by:	Length:
Columbia	Jimmy Driftwood	2 mins 28 secs

John LaGale 'Johnny' Horton (b. April 30, 1925 - d. November 5, 1960) was a country music and rockabilly singer, and musician. He was best known for his saga ballads such as the 'The Battle Of New Orleans' which was awarded the 1960 Grammy Award for Best Country & Western Recording. Horton died in November 1960 at the peak of his fame in an automobile accident, less than two years after his breakthrough. He is a member of the Rockabilly Hall of Fame and the Louisiana Music Hall of Fame.

Bobby Darin
Mack The Knife

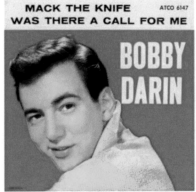

Label:	Written by:	Length:
ATCO Records	Brecht / Weill / Blitzstein	3 mins 4 secs

Bobby Darin (b. Walden Robert Cassotto; May 14, 1936 - d. December 20, 1973) was a singer, songwriter, multi-instrumentalist, and actor in film and television. He performed jazz, pop, rock and roll, folk, swing, and country music. He started his career as a songwriter for Connie Francis and recorded his first million-selling single 'Splish Splash' in 1958. This 1959 U.S. and U.K. No.1 hit earned Darin a Grammy Award for Record Of The Year.

③ Lloyd Price
Personality

Label:
ABC-Paramount

Written by:
Logan / Price

Length:
2 mins 35 secs

Lloyd Price (b. March 9, 1933) is an R&B vocalist known as 'Mr. Personality'. Although his first recording Lawdy Miss Clawdy was a hit in 1952 it wasn't until the late 1950s that he achieved a series of national hits including Stagger Lee, Personality, and I'm Gonna Get Married. Price was inducted into the Rock and Roll Hall of Fame in 1998 and in 2010 (on 77th birthday) was inducted into the Louisiana Music Hall of Fame.

---

④ Frankie Avalon
Venus

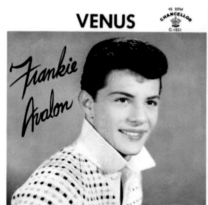

Label:
Chancellor

Written by:
Ed Marshall

Length:
2 mins 21 secs

Frankie Avalon (b. Francis Thomas Avallone; September 18, 1939) is an Italian-American actor, singer, and former teen idol. Avalon had 31 charted U.S. Billboard singles from 1958 to late 1962, which included two No.1 hits, Venus and Why (both in 1959). In 1976 Avalon released a new disco version of Venus which peaked at No.46 on the U.S. Billboard Hot 100 Chart and at No.1 on the Easy Listening Chart.

5 Paul Anka
Lonely Boy

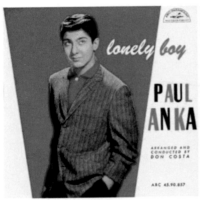  

| **Label:** | **Written by:** | **Length:** |
| ABC-Paramount | Paul Anka | 2 mins 33 secs |

Paul Albert Anka (b. July 30, 1941) is a Canadian-American singer, songwriter, and actor. Anka became famous during the late 1950s, 1960s and 1970s with hit songs like Diana, Lonely Boy, Put Your Head On My Shoulder and (You're) Having My Baby. He also wrote one of Tom Jones's biggest hits, She's A Lady, as well as the English lyrics for Frank Sinatra's signature song, My Way. Anka was inducted into the Canadian Music Hall of Fame in 1980.

---

6 Bobby Darin
Dream Lover

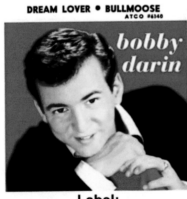  

| **Label:** | **Written by:** | **Length:** |
| ATCO Records | Bobby Darin | 2 mins 28 secs |

Dream Lover was written by Bobby Darin and recorded by him on April 6, 1959. It was released as a single on Atco Records and became a multi-million seller, reaching No.2 on the U.S. charts for a week and No.4 on the R&B charts; it was kept from the No.1 spot by 'The Battle Of New Orleans' by Johnny Horton - it did however reach No.1 in the U.K. for four weeks during June and July 1959. In addition to Darin's vocals the song also features Neil Sedaka on piano.

7 The Browns
The Three Bells

Label:
RCA Victor

Written by:
Reisfeld / Villard

Length:
2 mins 47 secs

The Browns were a country and folk music vocal trio best known for their Grammy-nominated hit, The Three Bells. The group, composed of Jim Edward Brown (b. April 1, 1934 - d. June 11, 2015) and his sisters Maxine born (b. April 27, 1932) and Bonnie (b. July 31, 1938 - d. July 16, 2016), had a close smooth harmony which was characteristic of the Nashville sound, though their music also combined elements of folk and pop. They disbanded in 1967 and were recently elected to the Country Music Hall of Fame (March 2015).

---

8 The Fleetwoods
Come Softly To Me

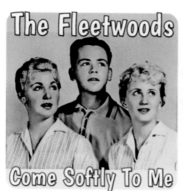

Label:
Dolphin

Written by:
Ellis / Troxel / Christopher

Length:
2 mins 25 secs

The Fleetwoods were a vocal trio from Olympia, Washington, consisting of members Gary Troxel (b. November 28, 1939), Gretchen Christopher (b. February 29, 1940), and Barbara Ellis (b. February 20, 1940). Their specialty was soft, romantic ballads. The groups' first record release, Come Softly To Me, became an instant hit and reached No.1 on the U.S. pop charts. The Fleetwoods were inducted into both the Vocal Group Hall of Fame and the Doo-Wop Hall of Fame of America in 2006..

Wilbert Harrison
Kansas City

Label:	**Written by:**	**Length:**
Fury Records	Stoller / Leiber	2 mins 21 secs

Wilbert Huntington Harrison (b. January 5, 1929 - d. October 26, 1994) was a rhythm and blues singer, pianist, guitarist and harmonica player. Kansas City was written in 1952 and was one of the first credited collaborations by the team of Jerry Leiber and Mike Stoller; it sold over one million copies. The song was given a Grammy Hall of Fame Award and has also been named as one of the Rock and Roll Hall of Fame's 500 Songs that Shaped Rock and Roll. Harrison was inducted into the North Carolina Music Hall of Fame in 2009.

The Fleetwoods
Mr. Blue

Label:	**Written by:**	**Length:**
Dolton	DeWayne Blackwell	2 mins 26 secs

Mr. Blue was the third hit single by The Fleetwoods and their second and last No.1 recording. For the following three years The Fleetwoods had a string of minor pop hits. The group wasn't able to consistently place singles in the upper regions of the charts partially because Troxell was drafted into the Navy at the height of the group's popularity; during this time he was temporarily replaced by Vic Dana.

1959: TOP FILMS

1. **Ben-Hur** - *MGM*
2. **Operation Petticoat** - *Universal Pictures*
3. **Some Like It Hot** - *United Artists*
4. **The Shaggy Dog** - *Disney*
5. **Pillow Talk** - *Universal Pictures*

OSCARS

Best Picture: Ben-Hur

Best Director: William Wyler *(Ben-Hur)*

Best Actor:
Charlton Heston *(Ben-Hur)*

Best Actress:
Simone Signoret *(Room At The Top)*

Best Supporting Actor:
Hugh Griffith *(Ben-Hur)*

Best Supporting Actress:
Shelley Winters *(The Diary Of Anne Frank)*

BEN-HUR

THE ENTERTAINMENT EXPERIENCE OF A LIFETIME!

METRO-GOLDWYN-MAYER
presents

A Tale of the Christ
by GENERAL LEW WALLACE

BEN-HUR

Directed by
WILLIAM WYLER

Starring
CHARLTON HESTON · JACK HAWKINS
HAYA HARAREET · STEPHEN BOYD

Directed by: William Wyler - Runtime: 3 hours 32 minutes

A rich Jewish prince called Judah Ben-Hur is betrayed and sent into slavery by his old childhood friend Messala, the new Roman governor of Jerusalem. Judah regains his freedom and seeks revenge against his one-time friend.

STARRING

Charlton Heston
Born: October 4, 1923
Died: April 5, 2008

Character:
Judah Ben-Hur

Born John Charles Carter, Heston was an actor and political activist. As a Hollywood star he appeared in around 100 films over the course of 60 years. For his role as Moses in The Ten Commandments (1956) he received his first Golden Globe Award nomination and in 1959 won the Academy Award for Best Actor playing the titular character in Ben-Hur. Other notable films include El Cid (1961) and Planet Of The Apes (1968).

Jack Hawkins, CBE
Born: September 14, 1910
Died: July 18, 1973

Character:
Quintus Arrius

Actor who worked on stage and in film. He made his London stage debut aged eleven playing the Elf King in Where The Rainbow Ends (December 1923). Hawkins was one of the most popular British film stars of the 1950s and was best known for his portrayal of military men in films like, Angels One Five (1951), The Cruel Sea (1953), Bridge On The River Kwai (1957), Ben-Hur and Lawrence Of Arabia (1962).

Haya Harareet
Born: September 20, 1931

Character:
Esther

Israeli actress who is perhaps best known for playing Esther, Charlton Heston's love interest in Ben-Hur. Harareet began her career in Israeli films with Hill 24 Doesn't Answer (1955), which was nominated for the Palme d'Or at the 1955 Cannes Film Festival. During her career she appeared in just a handful of other films including The Doll That Took The Town (1957), L'Atlantide (1961), The Secret Partner (1961) and The Interns (1962).

TRIVIA

Goofs Sheik Ilderim pins a Star of David onto Ben-Hur's belt before the chariot race, presumably in an attempt to goad the Romans. The Star of David didn't become a symbol of Judaism until the Middle Ages in Eastern Europe.

When Judah and Messala argue in the courtyard of Judah's home, road noise and honking horns from cars can be heard in the background. For some reason these were not removed from the soundtrack post production.

During the chariot race a Volkswagen Beetle can be seen in the background.

CONTINUED

Interesting Facts

Ben-Hur is the first of three films to have won 11 Academy Awards; the second was Titanic (1997) and the third was The Lord of the Rings: The Return of the King (2003).

The chariot race required 15,000 extras on a set constructed on 18 acres of backlot at Cinecitta Studios outside Rome. Eighteen chariots were built, with half being used for practice. The race took five weeks to film.

Martha Scott was 45 years old at the time of filming, only ten years older than her screen son Charlton Heston. Three years previously she also played Heston's mother in The Ten Commandments (1956).

Paul Newman was offered the role of Judah Ben-Hur but turned it down because he'd already done one Biblical-era film, The Silver Chalice (1954), and hated the experience. He also said it taught him that he didn't have the legs to wear a tunic.

During an 18-day auction of MGM props, costumes and memorabilia in May 1970, a Sacramento restaurateur paid $4,000 for a chariot used in the film. Three years later, during the energy crisis, he was arrested for driving the chariot on the highway.

Ben-Hur is the only Hollywood film to make the Vatican approved film list in the category of religion.

Quote

Sextus: You can break a man's skull, you can arrest him, you can throw him into a dungeon. But how do you control what's up here?
[taps his head]
Sextus: How do you fight an idea?

OPERATION PETTICOAT

CARY GRANT ★ TONY CURTIS

OPERATION PETTICOAT

in Eastman COLOR

Co-starring
JOAN O'BRIEN · DINA MERRILL · GENE EVANS with DICK SARGENT
and ARTHUR O'CONNELL

Directed by: Blake Edwards - Runtime: 2 hours 4 minutes

During World War II a commander finds himself stuck with a decrepit (pink) submarine, a staff officer with no discernible naval experience and a group of army nurses.

STARRING

Cary Grant
Born: January 18, 1904
Died: November 29, 1986

Character:
Lt. Cmdr. Matt T. Sherman

British-American actor known as one of classic Hollywood's definitive leading men. He began a career in Hollywood in the early 1930s and became known for his transatlantic accent, light-hearted approach to acting, comic timing and debonair demeanour. He was twice nominated for the Academy Award for Best Actor for his roles in Penny Serenade (1941) and None But The Lonely Heart (1944); in 1970 he was given an Honorary Oscar for Lifetime Achievement.

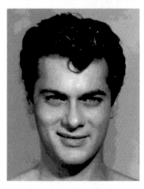

Tony Curtis
Born: June 3, 1925
Died: September 29, 2010

Character:
Lt. JG Nicholas Holden

Actor born Bernard Schwartz whose career spanned six decades. He appeared in more than 100 films throughout his career, in roles covering a wide range of genres from light comedy to serious drama. Curtis was nominated for an Oscar for Best Actor in The Defiant Ones (1958) and starred in many other notable film roles including Some Like It Hot (1959), Operation Petticoat, Spartacus (1960), and The Boston Strangler (1968).

Joan O'Brien
Born: February 14, 1936

Character:
Lt. Dolores Crandall RN

Actress and singer who made a name for herself acting in television shows in the 1950s and 1960s. Her career began in 1949 when her singing abilities came to the attention of Cliffie Stone, who hired her as a regular performer on his television show Hometown Jamboree. O'Brien had a short film career (1958-1964) but during that time she co-starred with Cary Grant, Elvis Presley, John Wayne and Jerry Lewis. She retired from acting altogether in 1965.

TRIVIA

Goofs | The map on the office wall, where Cary Grant and his superior are discussing the damages to the submarine, is clearly a mid '50s world map. The borders of European countries are clearly post war and it shows both India and Pakistan; they didn't exist as separate countries until 1947.

When the station wagon crashes into the limousine the sound of the crash comes before the actual collision.

Interesting Facts | This was the second time Cary Grant played a submarine commander. The first was Destination Tokyo (1943).

CONTINUED

Interesting Facts The sinking of the truck in the movie was inspired by real incident that happened in 1944. On August 9, 1944, USS Bowfin (SS-287) followed four ships into Minami Daito Harbour. As she fired her six bow torpedoes at the moored ships, hitting three and sinking two of them, one torpedo went astray and hit a pier. A bus parked on it was blown up and thrown into the water by the explosion.

Bob Hope always said it was his biggest regret that he turned down this movie.

Tina Louise was offered but turned down the role of Nurse Crandall (eventually played by Joan O'Brien) because Louise didn't like the abundant boob jokes directed at the character.

Quotes **Lt. Cmdr. Matt T. Sherman**: When a girl is under 21, she's protected by law. When she's over 65, she's protected by nature. Anywhere in between, she's fair game. Look out.

Lt. Cmdr Matt T. Serman: Sir, Sea Tiger was built to fight. She deserves a better epitaph than 'Commissioned 1940, sunk 1941, engagements none, shots fired none.' Now, you can't let it go that way. That's like a beautiful woman dying an old maid, if you know what I mean by old maid.
Capt. J.B. Henderson: Did you ever sell used cars?
Lt. Cmdr. Matt T.Sherman: No, Sir.
Capt. J.B. Henderson: I've got a hunch you missed your calling.

SOME LIKE IT HOT

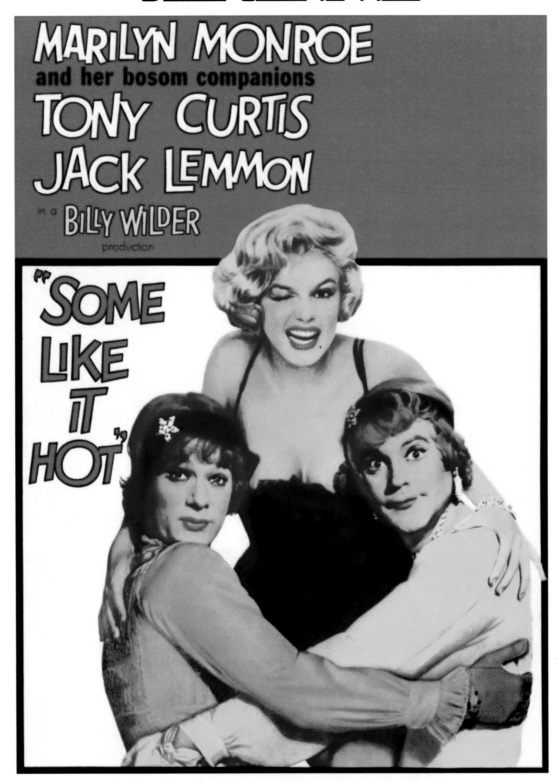

Directed by: Billy Wilder - Runtime: 2 hours 1 minute

When two male musicians witness a mob hit they flee the state in an all-female band disguised as women, but further complications set in.

STARRING

Marilyn Monroe
Born: June 1, 1926
Died: August 5, 1962

Character:
Sugar Kane Kowalczyk

Actress, model and singer born Norma Jeane Mortenson. Famous for playing comic 'blonde bombshell' characters, she became one of the most popular sex symbols of the 1950s and was emblematic of the era's attitudes towards sexuality. Although she was a top-billed actress for only a decade her films grossed $200 million by the time of her death in 1962. More than half a century later she continues to be a major popular cultural icon.

Tony Curtis
Born: June 3, 1925
Died: September 29, 2010

Characters:
Joe / Josephine

Actor born Bernard Schwartz whose career spanned six decades. He appeared in more than 100 films throughout his career, in roles covering a wide range of genres from light comedy to serious drama. Curtis was nominated for an Oscar for Best Actor in The Defiant Ones (1958) and starred in many other notable film roles including Some Like It Hot, Operation Petticoat (1959), Spartacus (1960), and The Boston Strangler (1968).

Jack Lemmon
Born: February 8, 1925
Died: June 27, 2001

Character:
Jerry / Daphne

Actor and musician who starred in over 60 films during his career. He was nominated eight times for an Academy Award, winning twice for his roles in Mister Roberts (1955) and Save The Tiger (1973). Lemmon worked with many of the top actresses of the day including Marilyn Monroe, Natalie Wood, Betty Grable, Janet Leigh, Shirley MacLaine, Doris Day, Rita Hayworth, Ann-Margret and Sophia Loren.

TRIVIA

Goofs	As the band members are organizing the party in Daphne's berth, the girl bringing the cheese and crackers is holding a jar of Cheez Whiz. The film is set in 1929, and Cheez Whiz was not introduced to the market until around 1952.
	As Sweet Sue addresses the ballroom audience we hear strings only, yet the brass section behind her is playing.
Interesting Facts	Upon the film's original release the state of Kansas banned it from being shown because they believed people from Kansas would find cross-dressing 'too disturbing'.

CONTINUED

Interesting Facts

Jerry Lewis was offered the role of Jerry/Daphne but declined because he didn't want to dress in drag. When Jack Lemmon received an Oscar nomination for the role Lewis claims Lemmon sent him chocolates every year to thank him.

Marilyn Monroe required 47 takes to get "It's me, Sugar" correct, instead saying either "Sugar, it's me" or "It's Sugar, me". After take 30, Billy Wilder had the line written on a blackboard. Another scene required Monroe to rummage through some drawers and say "Where's the bourbon?" After 40 takes of her saying "Where's the whiskey?", 'Where's the bottle?', or "Where's the bonbon?", Wilder pasted the correct line in one of the drawers. After Monroe became confused about which drawer contained the line, Wilder had it pasted in every drawer. Fifty-nine takes were required for this scene and when she finally does say it, she has her back to the camera, leading some to wonder if Wilder finally gave up and had it dubbed.

A male cabaret dancer named Babette tried to teach Tony Curtis and Jack Lemmon to walk in heels. After about a week Lemmon declined his help saying he didn't want to walk like a woman, but as a man trying to walk like a woman.

Supposedly when Orry-Kelly was measuring all three stars for dresses, he half-jokingly told Marilyn Monroe, "Tony Curtis has a nicer butt than you," at which point Monroe pulled open her blouse and said, "Yeah, but he doesn't have tits like these!"

Quotes

Jerry: Have I got things to tell you!
Joe: What happened?
Jerry: I'm engaged.
Joe: Congratulations. Who's the lucky girl?
Jerry: I am!

Sugar: Real diamonds! They must be worth their weight in gold!

Sugar: Oh, Daphne, how can I ever repay you?
Jerry: Oh, I can think of a million things.
[Sugar gets into bed with him]
Jerry: And that's one of them!

THE SHAGGY DOG

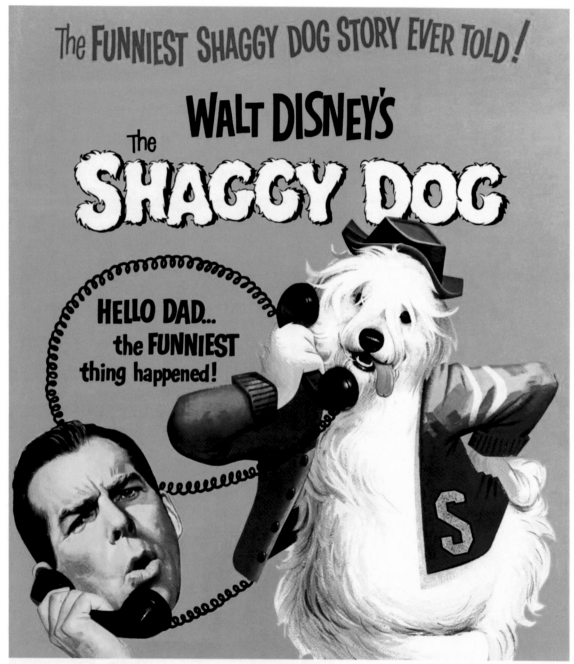

Directed by: Charles Barton - Runtime: 1 hour 44 minutes

An ancient spell causes a boy to keep transforming into a sheepdog at the most inopportune times. It appears that the spell can only be broken through a heroic act of selflessness...

STARRING

Fred MacMurray
Born: August 30, 1908
Died: November 5, 1991

Character:
Wilson Daniels

Actor who appeared in more than 100 films during a career that spanned nearly half a century. MacMurray is best known for his roles in the film Double Indemnity (1944) and for his performances in numerous Disney films including The Shaggy Dog, The Absent-Minded Professor (1961) and The Happiest Millionaire (1967). In 1960 he took the role of Steve Douglas, the widowed patriarch on My Three Sons, which ran on ABC and CBS until 1972.

Jean Hagen
Born: August 3, 1923
Died: August 29, 1977

Character:
Freeda Daniels

Actress, born Jean Shirley Verhagen, who began her show business career on radio in the 1940s. She is best known for her role as Lina Lamont in Singin' In The Rain (1952) for which she was nominated for an Academy Award for Best Supporting Actress. Hagen was also nominated three times for an Emmy Award for Best Supporting Actress in a Comedy Series for her role as Margaret Williams on the television series Make Room For Daddy (1953-1956).

Tommy Kirk
Born: December 10, 1941

Character:
Wilby Daniels

A former actor and later a businessman. He is best known for his performances in a number of highly popular movies made by Walt Disney Studios such as, Old Yeller (1957), The Shaggy Dog, The Swiss Family Robinson (1960) and The Misadventures Of Merlin Jones (1964), as well as beach-party movies of the mid-1960s. Kirk was inducted as a Disney Legend for his work in film and television on October 9, 2006.

TRIVIA

Goofs In the scene where the boys launch the missile interceptor, the dining room's furnishings (the vase and cabinet behind Fred MacMurray) start to shake before the rocket is even ignited.

Immediately after Franceska cleans the cut above Buzz Miller's eye the cut disappears.

Interesting Facts The words Wilby Daniels recites from the ring to turn himself in to a shaggy dog are 'in canis corpore transmuto' (latin for 'I transmute into the body of a dog').

CONTINUED

Interesting Facts

This was the first live-action feature comedy produced by Walt Disney.

As a kind of product placement for Walt Disney's associate publisher Dell, a character is seen reading an Uncle Scrooge comic dated June 1957. This issue (No.18) features the Carl Barks-written adventure 'Land Of The Pygmy Indians'.

Gregory Peck was the second choice for the role of Wilson Daniels.

Although she gets billing above Tim Considine and Roberta Shore, Annette Funicello (in her film debut) has a much smaller role than they do.

This was the first of six Walt Disney films starring Fred MacMurray.

Quotes

Wilby Daniels: What about the seven bucks I loaned you?
Buzz Miller: What about it?
Wilby Daniels: Cough it up. Pop pulled the plug on my allowance.
Buzz Miller: Gee, pal, I'd like to help you out, but you know how it is. I've got a date with Allison.
Wilby Daniels: I'm sick and tired of financing your romances.

Moochie Daniels: Gee, Wilby, you know I like you much better as a dog.

PILLOW TALK

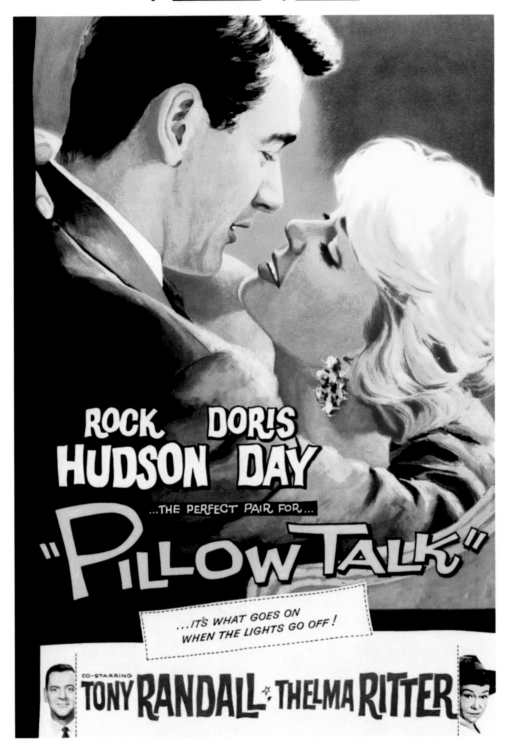

Directed by: Michael Gordon - Runtime: 1 hour 42 minutes

Playboy songwriter Brad Allen's succession of romances annoys his neighbor, interior designer Jan Morrow, who shares a telephone party line with him and hears all his breezy routines. After Jan unsuccessfully lodges a complaint against him, Brad sets about to seduce her in the guise of an upstanding Texas rancher.

STARRING

Rock Hudson
Born: November 17, 1925
Died: October 2, 1985

Character:
Brad Allen

Actor and heartthrob generally known for his roles as a leading man in films during the 1950s and 1960s. He first achieved stardom in films such as Magnificent Obsession (1954), All That Heaven Allows (1955) and Giant (1956). Hudson later found continued success with a string of romantic comedies co-starring Doris Day. In total he starred in nearly 70 films and several television productions during a career that spanned over four decades.

Doris Day
Born: April 3, 1922

Character:
Jan Morrow

An actress, singer, and animal welfare activist born Doris Mary Ann Kappelhoff. After she began her career as a big band singer in 1939 her popularity increased with her first hit recording, Sentimental Journey (1945). She recorded more than 650 songs from 1947 to 1967, becoming one of the most popular and acclaimed singers of the 20th century. Day's film career began with Romance On The High Seas (1948) and its success sparked a 20 year career as a motion picture actress.

Tony Randall
Born: February 26, 1920
Died: May 17, 2004

Characters:
Jonathan Forbes

Actor, born Aryeh Leonard Rosenberg, who is best known for his role as Felix Unger in a television adaptation of the 1965 play The Odd Couple by Neil Simon. In a career spanning around 6 decades, Randall received 6 Golden Globe Award nominations and 6 Primetime Emmy Award nominations (winning one in 1975 for his work on the sitcom The Odd Couple). In 1991, Randall founded the National Actors Theatre at Pace University in New York City.

TRIVIA

Goofs	When Jan and Jonathan are talking in front of the interior design store about the car he is offering her, the same extras are seen multiple times. A woman with a blue coat and gray hat walks by 4 times, and a woman with a red coat walks by at least 3 times.
	When Brad sees his re-decorated apartment, the cat continues to meow even though its mouth is closed.
Interesting Facts	Doris Day acknowledged that this movie transformed her image from 'the girl next door' to classy sophisticated sex symbol, as the plot for its time was quite racy.

Interesting Facts | This movie would be the first of three to showcase the trio of Doris Day, Rock Hudson and Tony Randall all together; it was followed by Lover Come Back (1961) and Send Me No Flowers (1964).

Rock Hudson turned down the film three times believing the script to be too risqué. Doris Day finally talked him into starring in it and it subsequently became one of his biggest hits.

Pillow Talk earned Doris Day her only Oscar nomination.

Spanish TV screened Pillow Talk on July 20, 1969, while everybody was waiting for the Apollo moon landing - it was then stopped suddenly so Spanish people could watch the landing live. The film was not reshown again until 1999, when Spanish viewers could, at last, see the ending.

Quotes | **Jan**: Officer, arrest this man - he's taking me up to his apartment!
Police Officer: Well, I can't say that I blame him, miss.

Jonathan Forbes: Brad, she is the sweetest, she is the loveliest, she is the most talented woman I have ever met.
Brad Allen: That's what you said when you married that stripper.
Jonathan Forbes: She wasn't a stripper. She was an exotic dancer... with trained doves.

SPORTING WINNERS

INGEMAR JOHANSSON - BOXING

AP Associated Press - MALE ATHLETE OF THE YEAR

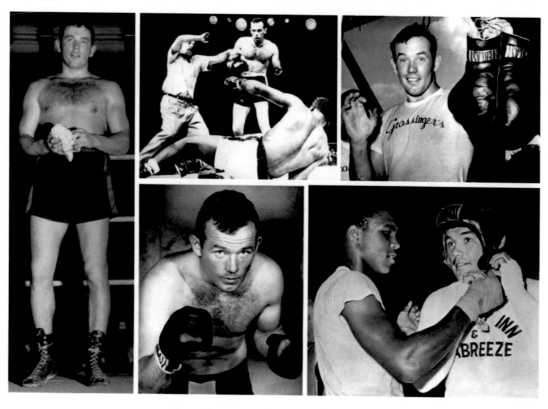

Jens Ingemar 'Ingo' Johansson
Born: September 22, 1932 in Gothenburg, Sweden
Died: January 30, 2009 in Kungsbacka, Sweden
Heavyweight Boxer - Height: 6ft 0in / Reach: 72in

Ingemar Johansson was a Swedish professional boxer who competed from 1952 to 1963. He held the world heavyweight title from 1959 to 1960, and was the fifth heavyweight champion to be born outside the United States. Johansson won the title by defeating Floyd Patterson via third-round stoppage, after flooring him seven times in that round. For this achievement, Johansson was awarded the Hickok Belt as top professional athlete of the year - the only non-American to do so in the belt's entire 27-year existence - and was named the Associated Press Male Athlete of the Year and Sports Illustrated Sportsman of the Year.

Boxing Record	Fights	Wins	By KO	Losses
	28	26	17	2

Johansson held the European heavyweight title twice, from 1956 to 1958 and from 1962 to 1963, and as an amateur won a silver medal in the heavyweight division at the 1952 Summer Olympics. He affectionately named his right fist 'Toonder and Lightning' for its concussive power, but it was also alternatively known as Ingo's Bingo and the Hammer of Thor.

MARIA BUENO - TENNIS

AP Associated Press - FEMALE ATHLETE OF THE YEAR

Maria Esther Andion Bueno
Born: October 11, 1939 in São Paulo, Brazil
Died: June 8, 2018 in São Paulo, Brazil
Professional Tennis Career: 1950-1977

Maria Bueno was a Brazilian professional tennis player. During her career she won 19 Grand Slam titles making her the most successful South American female tennis player in history, and the only one to ever win Wimbledon. Bueno was the year-end No.1 ranked female player in 1959 and 1960, and became the first woman ever to win a calendar-year Grand Slam in doubles (all four majors in a year), three of them with Darlene Hard and one with Christine Truman.

Tennis Titles:

Grand Slam Singles	Wimbledon	1959 / 1960 / 1964
	U.S. Open	1959 / 1963 / 1964 / 1966
Grand Slam Doubles	Australian Open	1960
	French Open	1960
	Wimbledon	1958 / 1960 / 1963 / 1965 / 1966
	U.S. Open	1960 / 1962 / 1966 / 1968
Grand Slam Mixed Doubles	French Open	1960

In 1959, Correios do Brasil issued a postal stamp in recognition of her winning the Wimbledon Ladies Singles Championships and the Associated Press voted her Female Athlete of the Year. Other honors for Bueno include being inducted into the International Tennis Hall of Fame in 1978 and in 2015 having the centre court of the Olympic Tennis Centre in Rio de Janeiro named after her.

GOLF

THE MASTERS - ART WALL, JR.

The Masters Tournament is the first of the majors to be played each year and unlike the other major championships it is played at the same location - Augusta National Golf Club, Georgia. This was the 23rd Masters Tournament and was held April 2-5. Art Wall, Jr. shot a final round of 66 (-6), with birdies on five of the last six holes. This was Wall's only major title and he finished it one stroke ahead of the runner-up Cary Middlecoff (the 1955 champion). The total prize fund was $76,100 with $15,000 going to the winner.

PGA CHAMPIONSHIP - BOB ROSBURG

The 1959 and 41st PGA Championship was played July 30 to August 2 at Minneapolis Golf Club in St. Louis Park, Minnesota, a suburb west of Minneapolis. Six strokes back at the start of the final round, Bob Rosburg shot a 66 (-4) to win his only major championship, one stroke ahead of runners-up Jerry Barber and Doug Sanders. The total prize fund was $51,175 of which $8,250 went to the champion Rosburg.

U.S. OPEN - BILLY CASPER

The 1959 U.S. Open Championship (established in 1895) was held June 11-14 at the Winged Foot Golf Club in Mamaroneck, New York, a suburb northeast of New York City. Billy Casper won the title one a stroke ahead of runner-up Bob Rosburg on the West Course. It was the first of Casper's three major titles, which included the 1966 U.S. Open and the Masters in 1970. The total prize fund was $49,200 with Casper taking home $12,000.

Billy Casper

Bob Rosburg

Art Wall, Jr.

WORLD SERIES - LOS ANGELES DODGERS

Los Angeles Dodgers   4 - 2   **Chicago White Sox**

Total attendance: 420,784 - Average attendance: 70,131
Winning player's share: $11,231 - Losing player's share: $7,257

The World Series is the annual championship series of Major League Baseball. Played since 1903 between the American League and the National League champion teams, it is determined through a best-of-seven playoff.

The 1959 World Series featured the National League champions, the Los Angeles Dodgers, beating the American League champions, the Chicago White Sox, four games to two. Each of the three games played at the Los Angeles Memorial Coliseum drew record crowds, with Game 5's attendance of 92,706 continuing to be a World Series record to this day. It was the Dodgers' second World Series victory in five years, their first in Los Angeles, and marked the first championship for a West Coast team.

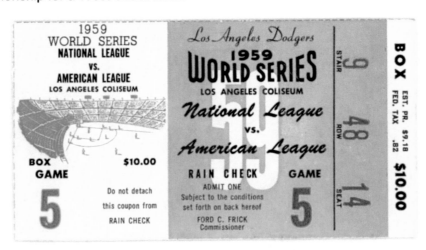

	Date	Score			Location	Time	Att.
1	Oct 1	Dodgers	0-11	**White Sox**	Comiskey Park	2:35	48,013
2	Oct 2	**Dodgers**	4-3	White Sox	Comiskey Park	2:21	47,368
3	Oct 4	White Sox	1-3	**Dodgers**	L.A. Memorial Coliseum	2:33	92,394
4	Oct 5	White Sox	4-5	**Dodgers**	L.A. Memorial Coliseum	2:30	92,650
5	Oct 6	**White Sox**	1-0	Dodgers	L.A. Memorial Coliseum	2:28	92,706
6	Oct 8	**Dodgers**	9-3	White Sox	Comiskey Park	2:33	47,653

Horse Racing

Sword Dancer with owner Isabel Dodge Sloane after his Belmont Stakes win.

Sword Dancer (April 24, 1956 - November 16, 1984) was an American Hall of Fame Champion Thoroughbred racehorse. He was the leading American colt of his generation and was voted United States Horse of the Year in 1959. He was a small chestnut horse, bred and owned by Isabel Dodge Sloane's Brookmeade Stable, and trained by J. Elliott Burch. In the 1959 Classic races Sword Dancer came second in both the Kentucky Derby and Preakness stakes, before winning the Belmont Stakes. During his racing career he ran in a total of 39 races of which he won 15; his total earnings were $829,610.

Kentucky Derby - Tomy Lee

The Kentucky Derby is held annually at Churchill Downs in Louisville, Kentucky on the first Saturday in May. The race is a Grade 1 stakes race for three-year-olds and is one and a quarter miles in length.

Preakness Stakes - Royal Orbit

The Preakness Stakes is held on the third Saturday in May each year at Pimlico Race Course in Baltimore, Maryland. It is a Grade 1 race run over a distance of 9.5 furlongs (1 3/16 miles) on dirt.

Belmont Stakes - Sword Dancer

The Belmont Stakes is Grade 1 race held every June at Belmont Park in Elmont, New York. It is 1.5 miles in length and open to three-year-old thoroughbreds. It takes place on a Saturday between June 5 and June 11.

FOOTBALL - NFL CHAMPIONSHIP

CHAMPIONSHIP GAME

Baltimore Colts

31 - 16

New York Giants

Played: December 27, 1959 at Memorial Stadium, Baltimore, Maryland.
Attendance: 57,545 - Referee: Ron Gibbs
Winning player's share: $4,674 - Losing player's share: $3,083

The 1959 National Football League Championship Game was the 27th NFL championship game, and featured the Baltimore Colts (the defending champions) against the New York Giants. The game went down to the last quarter when the Colts, trailing 9-7, scored 24 straight points and eventually won 31-16.

Conference Results:

Eastern Conference

Team	P	W	L	T	PCT	PF	PA
New York Giants	**12**	**10**	**2**	**0**	**.833**	**284**	**170**
Cleveland Browns	12	7	5	0	.583	270	214
Philadelphia Eagles	12	7	5	0	.583	268	278
Pittsburgh Steelers	12	6	5	1	.545	257	216
Washington Redskins	12	3	9	0	.250	185	350
Chicago Cardinals	12	2	10	0	.167	234	324

Western Conference

Team	P	W	L	T	PCT	PF	PA
Baltimore Colts	**12**	**9**	**3**	**0**	**.750**	**374**	**251**
Chicago Bears	12	8	4	0	.667	252	196
Green Bay Packers	12	7	5	0	.583	248	246
San Francisco 49ers	12	7	5	0	.583	255	237
Detroit Lions	12	3	8	1	.273	203	275
Los Angeles Rams	12	2	10	0	.167	242	315

Note: The NFL did not officially count tie games in the standings until 1972.

League Leaders

Statistic	Name	Team	Yards
Passing	Johnny Unitas	Baltimore Colts	2899
Rushing	Jim Brown	Cleveland Browns	1329
Receiving	Raymond Berry	Baltimore Colts	959

Hockey: 1958-59 NHL Season

The 1958-59 NHL season was the 42nd season of the National Hockey League and included six teams each playing 70 games. The Montreal Canadiens were the Stanley Cup champions beating the Toronto Maple Leafs four games to one in the best-of-seven final series. This marked the fourth consecutive Stanley Cup win for the Canadiens; the first team to win four in a row.

Final Standings:

	Team	GP	W	L	T	GF	GA	Pts
1	**Montreal Canadiens**	70	39	18	13	258	158	91
2	Boston Bruins	70	32	29	9	205	215	73
3	Chicago Black Hawks	70	28	29	13	197	208	69
4	Toronto Maple Leafs	70	27	32	11	189	201	65
5	New York Rangers	70	26	32	12	201	217	64
6	Detroit Red Wings	70	25	37	8	167	218	58

Scoring Leaders:

	Player	Team	GP	Goals	Assists	Points	PIM
1	**Dickie Moore**	**Montreal Canadiens**	70	41	55	96	61
2	Jean Beliveau	Montreal Canadiens	64	45	46	91	67
3	Andy Bathgate	New York Rangers	70	40	48	88	48

Hart Trophy (Most Valuable Player): Andy Bathgate - New York Rangers
Vezina Trophy (Fewest Goals Allowed): Jacques Plante - Montreal Canadiens

Stanley Cup

Montreal Canadiens

4 - 1

Toronto Maple Leafs

Series Summary:

	Date	Home Team	Result	Road Team
1	April 9	Toronto Maple Leafs	3-5	**Montreal Canadiens**
2	April 11	Toronto Maple Leafs	1-3	**Montreal Canadiens**
3	April 14	Montreal Canadiens	2-3	**Toronto Maple Leafs**
4	April 16	**Montreal Canadiens**	3-2	Toronto Maple Leafs
5	April 18	Toronto Maple Leafs	3-5	**Montreal Canadiens**

INDIANAPOLIS 500 - RODGER WARD

Rodger Ward in his Indy 500 winning Leader Card 500 Roadster.

The 43rd International 500-Mile Sweepstakes Race was held at the Indianapolis Motor Speedway on Saturday, May 30, 1959. The race was won by Rodger Ward, the first of his two career Indy 500 victories, in front of a crowd of 180,000 spectators. A record sixteen cars completed the full 500 miles and for the first time all cars were required to have roll bars.

Rodger M. Ward (b. January 10, 1921 - d. July 5, 2004) had 26 victories in top echelon open-wheel racing in North America. In 1992, he was inducted into the International Motorsports Hall of Fame and in 1995 was inducted in the Motorsports Hall of Fame of America.

BOSTON MARATHON
EINO OKSANEN

The Boston Marathon is the oldest annual marathon in the world and dates back to 1897. It is always held on Patriots' Day, the third Monday of April, and was inspired by the success of the first marathon competition at the 1896 Summer Olympics. The 1959 running of this race saw Helsinki police detective Eino Oksanen claim the first of his three Boston wins; he won it again in 1961 and 1962.

Race Result:

Pos.	Competitor	Country	Time
1.	**Eino Oksanen**	**Finland**	**2:22:42**
2.	John J. Kelley	United States	2:23:43
3.	Gordon Dickson	Canada	2:24:04

BASKETBALL - NBA FINALS

Boston Celtics

4 - 0

Minneapolis Lakers

Series Summary

	Date	Home Team	Result	Road Team
Game 1	April 4	**Boston Celtics**	118-115	Minneapolis Lakers
Game 2	April 5	**Boston Celtics**	128-108	Minneapolis Lakers
Game 3	April 7	Minneapolis Lakers	110-123	**Boston Celtics**
Game 4	April 9	Minneapolis Lakers	113-118	**Boston Celtics**

The 1959 NBA World Championship Series was a best-of-seven series which pitted the Western Division champion, Minneapolis Lakers, against the Eastern Division champion, Boston Celtics. The Boston Celtics swept the Lakers 4-0, and started what would become a run of 8 consecutive championships (1959-1966).

LEAGUE SUMMARY

Pos.	Eastern Division	W	L	PCT	Western Division	W	L	PCT
1	**Boston Celtics**	**52**	**20**	**.722**	St. Louis Hawks	49	23	.681
2	New York Knicks	40	32	.556	**Minneapolis Lakers**	**33**	**39**	**.458**
3	Syracuse Nationals	35	37	.486	Detroit Pistons	28	44	.389
4	Philadelphia Warriors	32	40	.444	Cincinnati Royals	19	53	.264

Division Finals Winners: Boston Celtics / Minneapolis Lakers

Statistics Leaders

	Player	Team	Stats
Points	Bob Pettit	St. Louis Hawks	2,105
Rebounds	Bill Russell	Boston Celtics	1,612
Assists	Bob Cousy	Boston Celtics	557
FG%	Kenny Sears	New York Knicks	.490
FT%	Bill Sharman	Boston Celtics	.932

Note: Prior to the 1969-70 season league leaders in points, rebounds and assists were determined by totals rather than averages.

TENNIS - U.S. NATIONAL CHAMPIONSHIPS

Maria Bueno and Neal Fraser in action, and posing with their U.S. Championship trophies.

Men's Singles Champion - Neale Fraser - Australia
Ladies Singles Champion - Maria Bueno - Brazil

The 1959 U.S. National Championships (now known as the U.S. Open) took place on the outdoor grass courts at the West Side Tennis Club, Forest Hills in New York. It was the 79th staging of the tournament and it ran from September 4 to September 13.

Men's Singles Final

Country	Player	Set 1	Set 2	Set 3	Set 4
Australia	Neale Fraser	6	5	6	6
United States	Alex Olmedo	3	7	2	4

Women's Singles Final

Country	Player	Set 1	Set 2
Brazil	Maria Bueno	6	6
United Kingdom	Christine Truman	1	4

Men's Doubles Final

Country	Players	Set 1	Set 2	Set 3	Set 4	Set 5
Australia	Neale Fraser / Roy Emerson	3	6	5	6	7
United States	Alex Olmedo / Earl Buchholz	6	3	7	4	5

Women's Doubles Final

Country	Players	Set 1	Set 2
United States	Jeanne Arth / Darlene Hard	6	6
United States	Althea Gibson / Sally Moore	2	3

Mixed Doubles Final

Country	Players	Set 1	Set 2	Set 3
United States / Australia	Margaret Osborne / Neale Fraser	7	13	6
United States / Australia	Janet Hopps / Bob Mark	5	15	2

THE COST OF LIVING

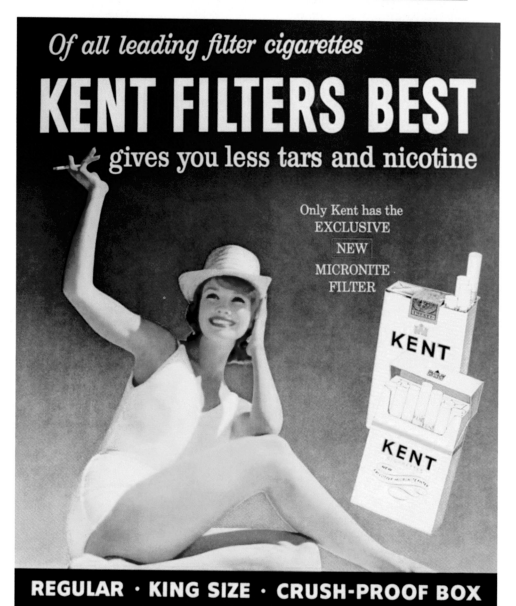

COMPARISON CHART

	1959 Price	1959 (+ Inflation)	2018 Price	% Change
Annual Income	$2,150	$18,618	$57,817	+210.5%
House	$18,500	$160,199	$295,000	+84.1%
Car	$2,750	$23,813	$33,560	+40.9%
Gallon Of Gasoline	31¢	$2.68	$2.43	-9.3%
Gallon Of Milk	37¢	$3.20	$4.42	+38.1%
DC Comic Book	10¢	87¢	$3.99	+358.6%

59

GROCERIES

Shady Lane Butter (1lb pkg.)	69¢
Shurfresh Margarine (1lb)	19¢
Deluxe Cheese Bread (loaf)	25¢
Boswell's Homo Milk (2x ½ gallon)	69¢
Large Country Eggs (dozen)	29¢
Shurfine Flour (5lb bag)	29¢
Aged Wisconsin Cheddar Cheese (per lb)	39¢
Lucerne Cottage Cheese (1lb cart.)	23¢
Sno-White Salt (3x 26oz pkgs.)	25¢
Peanut Butter (18oz jar)	39¢
Morton's Potato Chips (family size)	37¢
California Sunkist Oranges (per lb)	10¢
Bananas (per lb)	12¢
Potatoes No.1 Reds (10lb)	39¢
Fresh Green Cabbage (per lb)	5¢
Fresh Corn (4 ears)	25¢
Garden Fresh Green Onions (bun.)	5¢
T-Bone Steak (per lb)	85¢
Fresh Frosted Veal Cutlets (per lb)	89¢
Ground Beef (per lb)	39¢
Pork Roast Shoulder Butts (per lb)	39¢
Lone Star Pork Sausage (per lb)	19¢
Fresh Pig Liver (per lb)	19¢
Armour's Sliced Bacon (2lb cart.)	95¢
Skinless Frankfurters (per lb)	29¢
Fresh Dressed Hen (per lb)	29¢
Breaded Shrimp (10oz pkg.)	69¢
Del Monte Tuna (flat can)	35¢
Del Monte Catsup (2x 14oz bottle)	39¢
Blue Plate Mayonnaise	19¢
Speas White Vinegar (48oz)	45¢
Maxwell House Instant Coffee (6oz jar)	92¢
Coca-Cola (6 bottle cart.)	19¢
Shurfine Frozen Orange Juice (6oz can)	15¢
Tomato Juice (46oz can)	25¢
Lucky Leaf Apple Juice (32oz can)	29¢
Lustre-Creme Shampoo (large jar)	89¢
Max Factor Natural Curl	$1.50
Palmolive Soap (2 bath bars)	29¢
Barbasol Shave Cream (6oz can)	49¢
Tussy Stick Deodorant	50¢
Johnson's Talc	49¢
Chlorodent Toothpaste (x2)	73¢
Tide Washing Powder (giant size)	47¢
Zee Toilet Tissue (4 rolls)	34¢
Bayer Aspirin (100)	44¢
Pepto Bismol	89¢
Guardian Dog Food (3x 15¼oz cans)	27¢

PIGGLY WIGGLY'S
Pick of the Week Values

. . . A selection of finest foods in all departments, chosen to bring you top quality at lowest possible prices! For consistent savings, week after week, shop Piggly Wiggly! You'll find that even with their most exciting low prices, Piggly Wiggly never compromises with quality! If we can't have the best foods for you at sale prices -- we won't advertise the sale! So you can be sure of top values, better foods at Piggly Wiggly. Our quality is your greatest economy!

PICNICS Decker's Iowana— Smoked Whole 6 to 8-lb. Size ..... Lb. **25¢**

BACON Armour's Star Thick Sliced— Delicious For Boiling Or Frying **2** Lb. Pkg. **79¢**

PORK CHOPS First Cuts From Armour's 16 to 18-lb. Fresh Pork Loins— Buy USDA Inspected Meats From Your Piggly Wiggly ..... Lb. **37¢**

ARMOUR'S QUALITY BEEF
CHUCK ROAST ..... Lb. **39¢**

SNOWDRIFT 3-Lb. Can **49¢**

Morton's Potato Chips Large Family Size Package **39¢**

Morton's Corn Twistees ..... ¼-Lb. Pkg. **25¢**

Supreme Chocolate Fudge Sandwich **COOKIES** 1-Lb. Box **39¢** — Alcoa **FOIL** Regular Roll **35¢**

Supreme Club **CRACKERS** 1-Lb. Box **37¢** — Alma **Golden Corn** **2** No. 1 Cans **27¢**

Alma **SPAGHETTI** 300 Can **10¢** — Alma TURNIP **GREENS** **2** 303 Size **25¢**

TUNA Del Monte Chunk Style Reg. 35c Size ..... Only **29¢**

— GERBERS BABY FOODS —

STRAINED FOODS .. **4** Reg. Cans **35¢**

ORANGE JUICE ..... **2** 6-Oz. Cans **19¢**

Orange-Pineapple Juice **2** 6-Oz. Cans **19¢**

MIXED CEREAL ..... Reg. Pkg. **21¢**

OATMEAL CEREAL ..... Reg. Box **21¢**

COLORED HIGH GRADE
Speas Distilled Vinegar Quart Size **19¢**

Speas White Vinegar ..... 48-Oz. Size **45¢**

Speas APPLE CIDER Vinegar ..... Quart Size **29¢**

Palmolive Soap **2** Reg. Bars **21¢**

Palmolive Soap **2** Bath Size **29¢**

Cashmere Bouquet SOAP **3** Reg. Size **29¢**

FAB detergent Large Size **32¢**

VEL LIQUID 12-Oz. Can **41¢**

VEL detergent Giant Size **75¢**

DURKEE'S DEPENDABLE—
SNOW FLAKE
COCOANUT 7-Oz. Pkg. **29¢**

Shop Early For Your Xmas Baking!

FLOUR Pillsbury's Fine For All Your Baking! Extra Special **5** LB. BAG **29¢**

Bayer Aspirin 12 Size Box ..... **10¢**

HOSPITAL
RUBBING ALCOHOL PINT BOTTLE— (You Save 4c) ..... **15¢**

Ipana Tooth Paste Big Economy Size -- Only ..... (You Save 20c) **49¢**

U. S. NO. 1 GRADE—
POTATOES **10** -Lbs. **39¢**

YELLOW ONIONS Lb. **5¢**

Marvin Mince Meat ..... 9-Oz. Pkg. **27¢**

Del Monte Spinach **2** 303 Cans **33¢**

Towie Queen Olives Big 10-Oz. Jar **69¢**

Towie Cherries 8-Oz. Size Jar **35¢**

KARO SYRUP
Red Label ..... 5-Lb. Size **69¢**

Blue Label ..... 5-Lb. Can **69¢**

Green Label ..... 24-Oz. Size **27¢**

BOSCO Chocolate Syrup 24-Oz. Size **63¢**

Corn Oil Fine For All Cookies
MAZOLA OIL Quart Size **58¢**

Cashmere Bouquet SOAP **2** Bath Bars ..... **29¢**

VEL BEAUTY BAR **2** Reg. Bars ..... **37¢**

AJAX CLEANSER **2** Reg. Cans ..... **31¢**

AD Free Dinnerware In Each Package For Your Automatic Washing Machine. Giant Box ..... **83¢**

FLORIENT ROOM DEODORANT Assorted Reg. Can ..... **79¢**

Libbys Grade "A" Frozen
Orange Juice **2** 6-Oz. Cans **45¢**

CLOTHES

Women's Clothing

Sears Featherweight Coat	$7.99
R.J. Goldman Hats	$2.98 - $4.95
Pat & Babs Dresses	from $8.95
J.M. Dyer Shirtwaist Dress	$3.95
Lady Sutton Blouse	$1
Dollar Dept. Store Skirt	$1.77 - $2.77
Slim Jim Capri Pants	$1.99
Sears Nylon Slip	$4.98
Gossard Answer-Deb Girdle	$7.95
Macray's Nylonized Panties	19¢
Andrew Geller Black Patent Shoes	$24.95
K. Wolens Luxurious Leather Shoes	$4.99
Sears Rabbit Fur Slippers	$1.99

Men's Clothing

Suede Jacket	$19.75
P. Samuels Suburban Coat	$17.95
P. Samuels Felt Hat	$6.95
K. Wolens Summer Weight Flannel Suit	$29.95
Levine's White Linen Sports Coat	$12.99
K. Wolens White Shirt	$2.99
Macray's Short Sleeve Sport Shirt	97¢
Harris & Jacobs Wash 'n Wear Slacks	$8.95
Fine Broadcloth Pajamas	$2.99
Macray's Stretch Socks (pair)	29¢
Handkerchiefs (x3)	$1
Rabbit Fur Gloves	$3.98

TOYS

26 Inch Viking Bicycle - Boys Or Girls	$34.96
Electric Pinball Game	$19.98
Caster Horse	$3.79
Sears 5-Unit Allstate Electric Train Set	$17.88
2-Story Furnished Colonial Style Doll House	$6.98
11½ Inch Barbie Doll	$3
Tiny Tears Doll With Rock-A-Bye Eyes	$9.98
Plastic Bowling Set	$1.99
Battery Powered Remco Bull Dog Tank	$5.49
Mattel Cowboy Stagecoach Set	$7.99
Fort Apache Frontier Fort & Indian Camp	$5.99
Chrome Plated 3-PC Dinette	$14.99
Dolls 32-pc Dish Set	$1.99
21 Inch 'Bimbo' Plush Monkey	$2.98
Leather-Look Jewel Box	99¢
J.C. Higgins Rubber Basketball	$4.39
Official Football & Kicking Tee	$2.99
Genuine Willow Leather Baseball Glove	$3.44
Lou Burdette League Baseball	57¢

ELECTRICAL GOODS

Silvertone 21 Inch Table Model Television	$158.88
Speed Queen Automatic Washer	$229.95
Maytag Heavy Duty Dryer	$189
Westinghouse 1h.p. Air Conditioner	$169.95
General Electric Lightweight Iron	$7.95
Mirro Automatic Percolator	$8.95
Kenmore 12-Speed Table Mixer	$34.95
Westinghouse Portable Mixer	$14.28
Craftsman Drill	$10.88
6½ Inch Electric Handsaw	$34.95
Harmony House Electric Blanket	$15.88
Silvertone Portable Stereo Record Player	$99.88
All-Transistor Portable Radio	$19.99
Remington Rollectric Shaver	$18.95
Ronson Hair Dryer	$8.95

OTHER ITEMS

Lincoln Continental Mark 4	$7,056
Buick Invicta	$3,515
Studebaker Hawk	$2,630
NSU Prinz	$1,495
Allstate Silent Cushion 15 Inch Tires	$15.88
Allstate 6-Volt Car Batteries	$9.99
Firestone Criss Cross 4 Wheels & Balance	$6.99
20-Inch Dunlap Rotary Mower	$42.95
Eyes Examined / Glasses Fitted	from $12.50
Tower President XII Portable Typewriter	$115
Argus 3 Lens Movie Camera	$64.50
Brownie Turret Camera	$49.95
Joe York Hardwood 5-PC Dinette Set	$89.95
Enterprise Gas Range	$169.50
4-PC Sectional Sofa	$198
Sears 4½in Foam Latex Mattress	$77
Chatham Blanket	$5.95
W.M. House 10 Diamond Bridal Set	$124.50
W.M. House Diamond Solitaire Ring	$62.50
Birthstone Rings - 10 Karat Gold	$7.98
Elgin Sportsman Watch	$19.95
Leading Brands Cigarettes (pack)	39¢
Windproof Zippo Lighter	$3.50
Parker '21 Super' Pen Set	$8.95
Illustrated King James Leather Family Bible	$9.69

67

You're smoking better when it's Marlboro

U.S. COINS

Official Circulated U.S. Coins		Years Produced
Half-Cent	½¢	1793 - 1857
Cent - Penny	1¢	1793 - Present
2-Cent (Bronze)	2¢	1864 - 1873
3-Cent (Nickle)	3¢	1865 - 1889
Trime (3-Cent Silver)	3¢	1851 - 1873
Half-Dime	5¢	1794 - 1873
Five Cent Nickel	5¢	1866 - Present
Dime	10¢	1796 - Present
20-Cent	20¢	1875 - 1878
Quarter	25¢	1796 - Present
Half Dollar	50¢	1794 - Present
Dollar Coin	$1	1794 - Present
Gold Dollar	$1	1849 - 1889
Quarter Eagle	$2.50	1796 - 1929
Three-Dollar Piece	$3	1854 - 1889
Four-Dollar Piece	$4	1879 - 1880
Half Eagle	$5	1795 - 1929
Gold Eagle	$10	1795 - 1933
Double Eagle	$20	1849 - 1933
Half Union	$50	1915

*New Chrysler Windsor Convertible—
Chrysler quality at an economy price.*

SWEET TEMPTATION

...your lion-hearted '59 Chrysler!

*Chrysler's finest performer, the international
classic that's made in America—the 300-E.*

Chrysler convertibles are sunlight and adventure. In addition, their superb engineering and solid construction make them the most agile and confident cars on any road.

In Chrysler convertibles you get the entry ease of optional Swivel Seats . . . the instant action of Torque-Flite transmission . . . the safety of brawny Total-Contact Brakes . . . the economy of new Golden Lion engines . . . the control of Torsion-Aire Ride.

There are *three* new Chrysler convertibles. See them soon at your Chrysler dealer's.

lion-hearted
CHRYSLER
*. . . setting the pace
in style and comfort*

*Excitement and luxury go hand in
hand with the Chrysler New Yorker.*

CHRYSLER DIVISION OF CHRYSLER CORPORATION

COMIC STRIPS

BARNEY GOOGLE AND SNUFFY SMITH

BLONDIE

BARNEY GOOGLE AND SNUFFY SMITH

BLONDIE

70

Made in the USA
Lexington, KY
09 May 2019